JESUS

THE ONLY
WAY TO GOD

Other Books by John Piper

JESUS

THE ONLY
WAY TO GOD

Must You Hear the Gospel
to Be Saved?

JOHN PIPER

BakerBooks
a division of Baker Publishing Group
Grand Rapids, Michigan

© 2010 by Desiring God Foundation

Published by Baker Books
a division of Baker Publishing Group
P.O. Box 6287, Grand Rapids, MI 49516-6287
www.bakerbooks.com

Printed in the United States of America

Library of Congress Cataloging-in-Publication Data
Piper, John, 1946–
    Jesus: the only way to God : must you hear the gospel to be
saved? / John Piper.
        p.   cm.
    Includes bibliographical references.
    ISBN 978-0-8010-7263-5 (pbk.)
    1. Salvation—Christianity. 2. Jesus Christ—Person and offices.
I. Title.
BT751.3.P57 2010
232′.8—dc22   2010005226

10   11   12   13   14   15   16   7   6   5   4   3   2

Contents

5

Introduction

I have written this book with a sense of urgency. It seems to me that the very people who have historically been the most joyfully and sacrificially aggressive in world evangelization are losing their nerve. In our shrinking, pluralistic world, the belief that Jesus is the only way of salvation is increasingly called arrogant and even hateful. In the face of this criticism, many shrink back from affirming the global necessity of knowing and believing in Jesus.

There has always been a price to pay to take the good news of Jesus to those who need it and don't want it. The difference today is that those voices are closer to us than ever—whether in the neighborhood or on the internet. Their nearness makes them seem more numerous (which they aren't), and feel more dangerous (which they are).

These are not days for the timorous to open their mouths. A thousand bloggers stand ready to echo or condemn your commendation of Christ to a Jew, or Muslim, or Hindu, or Buddhist, or anyone else. Once upon a time, there was a safe, private place to take your controversial stand for Jesus. No more. If you are going to stand, you will be shot at—either figuratively or literally.

As I write this, there is news across the web of fourteen Christians killed in rioting because the other religion believed their holy book had been desecrated. What if, in your town, the "other" religion defined desecration as the public statement that their holy book is not the infallible guide to God?

The Commercialized, Psychologized Temperament

If the evangelical church at large was ever too confrontational in its evangelism, those days are gone. The pendulum has swung, with a commercialized and psychologized temperament, in the other direction. The church today leans strongly toward offering Jesus as appealing or not offering him at all. And what's new about this temperament is that we are more inclined than we used to be to let the customer, or the person who is offended, define what is appealing.

The commercialized mindset moves away from personal conviction toward pragmatic effectiveness. It feels that if the consumer is unhappy with the presentation, there must be something wrong with it. When this feeling becomes overriding, it circles around and redefines the "truth" being presented so that the presentation can be made enjoyable. If the claim that Jesus is the only way of salvation offends people, the commercialized mindset will either not talk about it or stop believing it.

The psychologized mindset defines love as whatever the other person feels is loving. The effect is the same as with the commercialized mindset. If a person or group finds your summons to believe on Jesus for salvation to be arrogant instead of humble and loving, then, if you have the psychologized mindset, you will feel guilty and apologetic. It must be your fault. If this mindset becomes overriding, it too will circle around and change not only the presentation, but, if necessary, the thing presented, so that the other person will not feel unloved.

In this way, the unhappy consumer and the offended listener take on a power that once belonged only to the Bible. There is an epidemic fear of man behind these two mindsets. In the name of marketing savvy or sensitive communication, cowardice capitulates to the world, and we surrender the offensive truth of Christ's uniqueness and supremacy.

What Is at Stake

My sense of urgency increases the more I think about what is at stake in surrendering the universal necessity of believing on Jesus in order to be saved. Consider these seven issues.

Believing and Obeying the Bible Is at Stake

Believing and obeying the Bible is at stake. Treating the Bible as our authority in matters of faith and practice is being lost in regard to the matter of people's destiny. Fearful squeamishness about what the Bible teaches is a bad sign in the church. It signifies a movement toward self, and away from God, as our authority.

The effects of this movement are not felt mainly in the first generation, because we still have enough of the residual effects of the Bible working in us for good. But in the next generation or two, the power of the Book will be broken and our children and grandchildren will be helpless in the riptides of popular culture.

"You will know the truth, and the truth will set you free" (John 8:32). "Sanctify them in the truth; your word is truth" (John 17:17). If we are cut loose from the anchor of God's Word, we will not be free. We will be slaves of personal passions and popular trends.

Genuine Love Is at Stake

Genuine love is at stake if we lose the universal uniqueness and supremacy of Jesus as the only way to God. "Love does no wrong to a neighbor; therefore love is the fulfilling of the law" (Rom. 13:10). But, oh, what a wrong we do to our neighbor if we neglect to take him the message that, by faith in Jesus, he will have everlasting life (John 3:16). The world will tell you that you are arrogant, not loving, if you spread the message of Jesus's saving work as the only way to God. But God calls it love.

The teaching that diminishes the urgency for reaching all the unreached peoples of the world with the only news that can save them is a teaching that *opposes* people. Listen to these severe words spoken by the apostle Paul about what it means to "oppose all mankind." He says that those who killed the Lord Jesus "drove us out, and displease God and oppose all mankind *by hindering us from speaking to the Gentiles that they might be saved*" (1 Thess. 2:14–16). This is what people do who tell us that the nations don't need to hear about Jesus in order to be saved. They oppose all mankind. Oh, how we need to let the Bible define what love does!

The Salvation of People in Other Religions Is at Stake

We will see over and over in the following pages that the salvation of people in other religions is at stake. They will not be saved by being sincere about their own faith. They will not be saved through the revelation of God in nature. The point of Romans 1:18–20 is that all people everywhere are without excuse in the judgment because, although God has revealed himself in nature, nevertheless fallen men "by their unrighteousness suppress the truth." Natural revelation does not save. It does not overcome this suppression. Only the gospel does.

God has appointed one way of salvation. Jesus Christ came into the world to save sinners (1 Tim. 1:15). There is one Mediator between God and men, the man Christ Jesus (1 Tim. 2:5). There is no other name but Jesus by which we must be saved (Acts

4:12). Jesus is the way, and no one comes to the Father but through him (John 14:6). All who call upon the name of Jesus will be saved, but they cannot call on the One they have not heard, and they cannot hear without a preacher (Rom. 10:13–14). What is at stake is the eternal salvation of perishing people.

The Strengthening of Missionaries Is at Stake

What is at stake as well is the encouragement and the empowering of thousands of missionaries, who are laying their lives down to reach people who have no access to the good news of Jesus. The teaching that people may be saved without hearing the gospel can rip the heart out of a missionary. There are already huge forces at work to undermine their faith, and destroy their joy, and ruin their ministry, and drag them home defeated. If we add this—that those who never hear about Jesus may be saved, no matter how we qualify it or nuance it—the devil himself will use it, if he can, to destroy his most feared and hated humans, the missionaries.

My aim here is to celebrate the immeasurably important work of missionaries. There is nothing like it in the world. Nothing can replace it. Oh, what a rare band—what a rare breed—of human beings are the pioneer missionaries who say with the apostle Paul, "I make it my ambition to preach the gospel, not where Christ has already been named, lest I build on someone else's foundation, but as it is written, 'Those who have never been told of him will see, and those who have never heard will understand'" (Rom. 15:20–21). The One whom the nations have never heard of, the One they will see when we tell them, is Jesus. In spite of all their sinfulness and ordinariness, there are no people more to be admired and encouraged than the missionaries who share this holy ambition.

Our Own Souls Are at Stake

At stake in this issue are our own souls. If we embrace a limitation on the universal necessity of the gospel to be heard and believed, we will begin to lose the gospel, and with it our own souls. When God appoints the gospel of his Son as the universal remedy for the guilt and corruption of mankind, and we diminish that, the gospel is diminished. And you cannot diminish the gospel without being diminished yourself. The spiritual health of the church hangs on her full-blooded gospel-engagement—with all its dangers and joys—in the mission of Jesus to gather his sheep from every religion and every language and every culture on the planet.

It is almost certain that cultural compromise and the fear of man are, in large measure, behind the abandonment of the dangerous doctrine of Jesus's global claim on the allegiance of every person. Therefore, if we surrender to this teaching, we embrace fear and conformity. It will not feel like fear and conformity, because the adversary will constantly tell us it is love and humility. But renaming a disease is no remedy. It goes on eating away at the soul, and will either lead to repentance or to more and more weakness. This is no small thing. Jesus is needed by the whole world for salvation. If we say otherwise, we strike a blow against our own conscience, and wound our soul.

The Enjoyment of All the Benefits of Christ Is at Stake

What is at stake in denying the necessity to hear and believe the good news of Jesus is not only the escape from hell, but the enjoyment of all the benefits of knowing Christ. This may seem obvious and even redundant. What else is the escape from hell but the entrance into God's presence and immeasurable pleasures at his right hand? But there are always cynics—even high-minded Christian cynics with motives too high, and aspirations too holy, to allow for a craven concern about hell—who remind us that there are greater goals in world missions than the "mere" escape from hell.

Well, there is no such thing as a "mere" escape from hell. Rescue from the worst and longest suffering can only be called "mere" by those who don't know what it is, or don't believe it's real. But implicit in the rescue from hell is the experience of praising God forever, and loving people forever, and enjoying creation forever, and creating beauty forever. All of this will be lost by everyone that the good news of Jesus does not reach. So what is at stake in diminishing the universal necessity of the gospel is the everlasting pleasures of people personally praising God, loving others, enjoying God's creation, and creating beauty. This is what people lose by not hearing and believing the gospel of Jesus.

The Glory of Jesus Is at Stake

This loss of pleasure means, in the end, that the glory of Jesus is at stake—at least in the limited sense of not shining brightly in the minds and hearts of those who deny the need for all to see it for salvation. But not only in that sense. God intends for the revelation of the glory of his Son to be the awakening of dead and blind hearts among all the peoples of the world. Everywhere in the world where the gospel has not spread, people suppress the truth about God and are blinded by Satan. "The god of this world has blinded the minds of the unbelievers" (2 Cor. 4:4).

What is the remedy for these blind eyes? They were made to see and admire Jesus—especially the glory of his grace manifest supremely in the cross and resurrection. Therefore, the remedy, in God's great wisdom, is the preaching of the cross by the people God sends. So Jesus says to Paul, "I am sending you to open their eyes, so that they may turn from darkness to light and from the power of Satan to God, that they may receive forgiveness of sins" (Acts 26:17–18). God opens the eyes of the blind when his spokesmen portray Jesus Christ. This is the work of the Holy Spirit in the world—to glorify Jesus (John 16:14).

Where Jesus is proclaimed as Lord and Savior and Treasure, God raises the spiritually dead and opens the eyes of the spiritually blind. And in that moment,

Christ is seen as glorious. He is trusted and treasured, and therefore honored. This is what is at stake, and why I have written this book.

May the Lord have mercy, and make it a means to motivate missions, magnify the necessity of the gospel, rescue the perishing, and glorify Jesus as the only way to God.

1

Is Jesus the Only Way of Salvation?

Three Questions in One

It is a stunning New Testament truth that since the incarnation of the Son of God in Jesus Christ, all saving faith is consciously focused on him. This was not always true. And those previous days Paul called *the times of ignorance*. "*The times of ignorance* God overlooked, but now he commands all people everywhere to repent, because he has fixed a day on which he will judge the world in righteousness *by a man* [Jesus Christ] whom he has appointed; and of this he has given assurance to all by raising him from the dead" (Acts 17:30–31).

But now it *is* true, and Christ is made the conscious center of the mission and the faith of the church. The aim of missions is to "bring about the obedience of faith *for the sake of his name* [the name of Jesus] among all the nations" (Rom. 1:5). This is a new thing with the coming of Christ. Since the incarnation, God's will is to glorify his Son by making him the conscious focus of all saving faith. Without this faith—faith resting consciously in Jesus as he is presented in the gospel— there is now no salvation.

That is what I believe the Bible teaches, and what I will be arguing in this book. As you can see, the implications are momentous. We are not dealing with a small matter. If this is true, the urgency of reaching unbelievers with the gospel is as great as it can be.

Three Questions in One

The general question that we often ask in regard to Christ and the other religions of the world, or in regard to those people who have never heard the gospel, is whether he is *the only way to salvation*. But that general question is ambiguous. It contains at least three questions. All of them are important for the missionary task of the Christian church.

The three questions will emerge if we listen to the way different people explain what they mean.

Question #1:
Will Anyone Experience Eternal, Conscious Torment under God's Wrath?

The first of the three questions is, "Will anyone experience eternal, conscious torment under God's wrath?" There are at least two ways of answering this question in the negative. One is to say that all people and devils will be saved eventually, and that hell, if it exists at all, will lead to repentance and purity and salvation. This approach is called *universalism*. The other is to say that those who are not saved are annihilated. They go out of existence rather than being cast into hell. This is known as *annihilationism*.

UNIVERSALISM

There is a personal side to this question for me. It is one thing to know that there are always "certain people" in the church who deny the reality of eternal hell, and it is another to love an author and then discover he is one of them. Since my college days, I had read three novels by George MacDonald: *Phantastes*, *Lilith*, and *Sir Gibbie*. I enjoyed them. I had also read a lot of C. S. Lewis and benefited immeasurably from the way he experienced the world and put that experience into writing.

I knew that Lewis loved MacDonald and commended him highly: "George MacDonald I had found for myself at the age of sixteen and never wavered in my allegiance."[1] "I have never concealed the fact that I regarded him as my master; indeed I fancy I have never written a book in which I did not quote from him."[2] "I know hardly any other writer who seems to

1. C. S. Lewis, "On the Reading of Old Books," in *God in the Dock: Essays on Theology and Ethics* (Grand Rapids: Eerdmans, 1970), 203.

2. C. S. Lewis, *George MacDonald: An Anthology* (London: Geoffrey Bles, 1946), 20.

be closer, or more continually close, to the Spirit of Christ Himself."[3]

Largely because of this remarkable advocacy by Lewis, I think, George MacDonald continues to have a significant following among American evangelicals. I certainly was among the number who was drawn to him. Then I picked up Rolland Hein's edition of *Creation in Christ*, a collection of MacDonald's sermons. To my great sorrow, I read these words: "From all the copies of Jonathan Edwards' portrait of God, however faded by time, however softened by the use of less glaring pigments, I turn with loathing."[4]

Those are strong words spoken about the God I had come to see in the Bible and to love. I read further and saw a profound rejection of the substitutionary atonement of Christ: "There must be an atonement, a making up, a bringing together—an atonement which, I say, cannot be made except by the man who has sinned."[5] And since only the man who has sinned can atone for his own sin (without a substitute), that is what hell is for.

MacDonald is a universalist not in denying the existence of hell, but in believing that the purpose of hell is to bring people to repentance and purity no matter how long it takes. "I believe that no hell will be lacking which would help the just mercy of God to redeem

3. Ibid., 18.

4. George MacDonald, *Creation in Christ: Unspoken Sermons,* ed. Rolland Hein (Wheaton: Harold Shaw, 1976), 81.

5. Ibid., 70.

His children."[6] And all humans are his children. If hell went on forever, he says, God would be defeated. "God is triumphantly defeated, I say, throughout the hell of His vengeance. Although against evil, it is but the vain and wasted cruelty of a tyrant."[7]

I mention George MacDonald as an example of a universalist not only because of my personal encounter with him but also because he represents the popular, thoughtful, artistic side of Christianity which continues to shape the way so many people think. A hundred years after MacDonald, another very popular Christian writer of fiction and award-winning children's books, Madeleine L'Engle (1918–2007), showed the influence of MacDonald. She wrote,

> I know a number of highly sensitive and intelligent people in my own communion who consider as a heresy my faith that God's loving concern for his creation will outlast all our willfulness and pride. No matter how many eons it takes, he will not rest until all of creation, including Satan, is reconciled to him, until there is no creature who cannot return his look of love with a joyful response of love.[8]

Both MacDonald and L'Engle reject the good news that Christ became a curse for us and bore the wrath of his Father in our place. Instead, they turn hell into an extended means of self-atonement and sanctifica-

6. Ibid., 77.
7. Ibid.
8. Madeleine L'Engle, *The Irrational Season* (New York: Seabury, 1977), 97.

tion. In hell the justice of God will eventually destroy all sin in his creatures. "Punishment is for the sake of amendment and atonement. God is bound by His love to punish sin in order to deliver His creature: He is bound by His justice to destroy sin in His creation."[9] In this way, God will bring everyone to glory. Everyone will be saved. Hell is not eternal.[10] All will be saved.[11]

ANNIHILATIONISM

Others would say that while not everyone is saved, there is still no eternal punishment because the fire of judgment annihilates those who reject Jesus. Thus they go out of existence and experience no conscious punishment. Hell is not a place of eternal punishment, but an event of annihilation.

For example, theologian Clark Pinnock says,

I was led to question the traditional belief in ever-lasting conscious torment because of moral revulsion and broader theological considerations, not

9. MacDonald, *Creation in Christ*, 72.

10. I have given an extended critique of MacDonald's view of divine justice, self-atonement, and universalism in *The Pleasures of God* (Sisters, OR: Multnomah, 2000), 168–74.

11. Years ago I interacted with a more philosophically sophisticated defense of the MacDonald position put forward by Thomas Talbott, who was professor of philosophy at Willamette University. His articles included "What Jesus Did for Us," *Reformed Journal* 40, no. 3 (March 1990): 8–12; "On Predestination, Reprobation, and the Love of God," *Reformed Journal* 33, no. 2 (February 1983): 11–14; "God's Unconditional Mercy—A Reply to John Piper," *Reformed Journal* 33, no. 6 (June 1983): 9–12. I responded to these last two articles with: "How Does a Sovereign God Love?" *Reformed Journal* 33, no. 4 (April 1983): 9–13; "Universalism in Romans 9–11? Testing the Exegesis of Thomas Talbott," *Reformed Journal* 33, no. 7 (July 1983): 11–14.

first of all on scriptural grounds. It just does not make any sense to say that a God of love will torture people forever for sins done in the context of a finite life. . . . It's time for evangelicals to come out and say that the biblical and morally appropriate doctrine of hell is annihilation, not everlasting torment.[12]

John Stott surprised and disappointed many of us in the late 1980s with a view that later he came to describe as agnostic on the question of annihilationism: "Emotionally, I find the concept [of eternal, conscious torment] intolerable and do not understand how people can live with it without either cauterizing their feelings or cracking under the strain." He gives four arguments that he says suggest that

Scripture points in the direction of annihilation, and that "eternal conscious torment" is a tradition which has to yield to the supreme authority of Scripture. . . . I do not dogmatize about the position to which I have come. I hold it tentatively. But I do plead for frank dialogue among Evangelicals on the basis of Scripture. I also believe that the ultimate annihilation of the wicked should at least be accepted as a legitimate, biblically founded alternative to their eternal conscious torment.[13]

12. Clark H. Pinnock and Delwin Brown, *Theological Crossfire: An Evangelical/Liberal Dialogue* (Grand Rapids: Zondervan, 1990), 226–27.

13. David Edwards, *Evangelical Essentials, with a Response from John Stott* (Downers Grove, IL: InterVarsity, 1988), 314–20. I will have more to say about Stott's position below and the interaction we had about this. For another annihilationist defense see also Edward William Fudge, *The Fire That*

So when we ask, "Is Jesus the only way to salvation?" we are asking the question: *Is he the only way to escape from an eternal conscious torment called hell?* So the question includes: Is there such a thing? Is eternal punishment at stake in the evangelization of the world? Will anyone be eternally cut off from Christ and experience eternal conscious torment under the wrath of God?

Question #2:
Is the Work of Christ Necessary for Salvation, or Are There Other Bases?

Another question embedded in the question "Is Jesus the only way to salvation?" is whether other religions also provide ways of salvation which are effective in leading people to eternal bliss, but are not based on the saving work of Christ. This is not the question about whether a person has to know about Jesus, but whether, known or not known, his work is the basis for all salvation.

All the people we mentioned so far in this chapter would agree that Christ's work *is* necessary. There would be no forgiveness of sin and no eternal life without it. But now we meet a more radical view, usually called "pluralism."[14] The pluralists believe that Jesus is

---

Consumes: The Biblical Case for Conditional Immortality, rev. ed. (Carlisle, UK: Paternoster, 1994).

14. Don Carson defines pluralism as "the view that all religions have the same moral and spiritual value, and offer the same potential for achieving salvation, however 'salvation' be construed" (D. A. Carson, *The Gagging of God* [Grand Rapids: Zondervan, 1996], 278–79).

the provision that God has made for Christians, but there are other ways of getting right with God and gaining eternal bliss in other religions. The work of Christ is useful for Christians but not necessary for non-Christians.

For example, British theologian John Hick argues that different religions are "equals, though they each may have different emphases." Christianity is not superior, but merely one partner in the quest for salvation. We are not to seek one world religion, but rather we look to the day when "the ecumenical spirit which has so largely transformed Christianity will increasingly affect relations between the world faiths." Hick quotes from the *Bhagavad Gita*, iv, 11, "Howsoever man may approach me, even so do I accept them; for, on all sides, whatever path they may choose is mine."[15]

Similarly John Parry, Other Faiths Secretary of the World Church and Mission Department of the United Reformed Church in London, wrote in 1985,

> It is to the faith *of* Jesus Christ that we are called. The change of preposition from *in* to *of* is significant. It is a faith that is shown in one's trust in God, in surrender to God's purposes, in giving oneself. Such a response of faith I have witnessed among my friends of other

15. John Hick, "Whatever Path Men Choose Is Mine," in *Christianity and Other Religions*, ed. John Hick and Brian Hebblethwaite (Philadelphia: Fortress, 1980), 188. For a survey of Hick's thoughts as well as a compelling response, see Harold Netland, *Dissonant Voices: Religious Pluralism and the Question of Truth* (Vancouver: Regent College Publishing, 1998), and Harold Netland, *Encountering Religious Pluralism: The Challenge to Christian Faith and Mission* (Downers Grove, IL: InterVarsity, 2001).

faiths. I cannot believe they are far from the kingdom of heaven; what is more, as Dr. Starkey writes, "People will not be judged for correct doctrinal beliefs but for their faith. Those who will enter the kingdom on the day of judgment are those who in faith respond to God's love by loving others."[16]

The position of pluralism means that the question we are asking must include: Is the work of Christ the necessary means provided by God for eternal salvation—not just for Christians, but for all people in all religions?

Question #3:
Is Conscious Faith in Christ Necessary for Salvation?

This brings us to the third question embedded in the general question of whether Jesus is the only way to salvation: "Is conscious faith in Christ necessary for salvation?" This is the question I am most concerned about because it is the one where more people are surrendering biblical truth. The view that says no to this question is usually called *inclusivism*. Don Carson defines it this way: "Inclusivism is the view that all who are saved are saved on account of the person and work of Jesus Christ, but that conscious faith in Jesus Christ is not absolutely necessary: some may be saved by him who have never heard of him, for they may respond positively to the light they have received."[17]

16. John Parry, "Exploring the Ways of God with Peoples of Faith," in *International Review of Mission* 74, no. 296 (October 1985): 512.

17. Carson, *Gagging of God*, 278.

For example, John Sanders says of the texts that seem to limit salvation to those who believe on Christ, "It is not certain from these passages that one must hear of Christ in this life to obtain salvation. They simply say there is no other way one can get to heaven except through the work of Christ; they do not say one has to know about that work in order to benefit from the work."[18]

Millard Erickson argues from Romans 1–2 and 10:18 that the revelation available in nature opens the way for people to be saved who have not heard of Christ. The essential elements of the "gospel message" in nature are:

(1) The belief in one good powerful God. (2) The belief that he (man) owes this God perfect obedience to his law. (3) The consciousness that he does not meet this standard, and therefore is guilty and condemned. (4) The realization that nothing he can offer God can compensate him (or atone) for this sin and guilt. (5) The belief that God is merciful, and will forgive and accept those who cast themselves on his mercy.

Then he asks,

May it not be that if a man believes and acts on this set of tenets he is redemptively related to God and receives the benefits of Christ's death, whether he consciously knows and understands the details

18. John E. Sanders, "Is Belief in Christ Necessary for Salvation?" *Evangelical Quarterly* 60 (1988): 246.

of that provision or not? Presumably that was the case with the Old Testament believers. . . . If this is possible, if Jews possessed salvation in the Old Testament era simply by virtue of having the form of the Christian gospel without its content, can this principle be extended? Could it be that those who ever since the time of Christ have had no opportunity to hear the gospel, as it has come through the special revelation, participate in this salvation on the same basis? On what other grounds could they fairly be held responsible for having or not having salvation (or faith)?

But here he is very tentative, for he goes on to say, "What Paul is saying in the remainder of Romans is that very few, if any, actually come to such a saving knowledge of God on the basis of natural revelation alone."[19]

Some scholars say we just don't know if or how God saves people who have never heard the gospel. For example, John Stott says, "I believe the most Christian stance is to remain agnostic on this question. . . . The fact is that God, alongside the most solemn warnings about our responsibility to respond to the gospel, has not revealed how he will deal with those who have never heard it."[20]

---

19. Millard Erickson, "Hope for Those Who Haven't Heard? Yes, But . . . ," *Evangelical Missions Quarterly* 11, no. 2 (April 1975): 124–25.

20. John Stott, quoted in David Edwards, *Evangelical Essentials*, 327. In the collection of essays edited by William V. Crockett and James G. Sigountos, *Through No Fault of Their Own* (Grand Rapids: Baker, 1991), Timothy Phillips, Aida Besancon Spencer, and Tite Tienou "prefer to leave the matter in the hands of God" (259n3).

So when we ask, "Is Jesus the only way to salvation?" we must make clear what we are really asking. One of the most important things we are asking is: *Is it necessary for people to hear of Christ in order to be eternally saved?* That is, can a person today be saved by the work of Christ even if he does not have an opportunity to hear about it and therefore never believes in Christ in this life?

In summary, then, we are asking three questions:

Question #1: Will anyone experience eternal conscious torment under God's wrath?

Question #2: Is the work of Christ necessary for salvation?

Question #3: Is conscious faith in Christ necessary for salvation?

A Nerve of Urgency

Biblical answers to these three questions are crucial because in each case a negative answer diminishes the urgency of the missionary cause. Evangelicals like Erickson do not intend to diminish that urgency, and their view is not in the same category with Hick or MacDonald. Those evangelicals insist that the salvation of anyone apart from the preaching of Christ would be the exception rather than the rule and that preaching Christ to all is utterly important.

Nevertheless, there is a felt difference in the urgency when one believes that preaching the gospel is absolutely the *only* hope that anyone has of escaping the penalty of sin and living forever in the happiness of God's presence. It does not ring true to me when William Crockett and James Sigountos argue that the existence of "implicit Christians" (saved through general revelation without hearing of Christ) actually "should increase motivation" for missions.

They say that these unevangelized converts are "waiting eagerly to hear more about [God]." If we would reach them, "a strong church would spring to life, giving glory to God and evangelizing their pagan neighbors."[21] I cannot escape the impression that this is a futile attempt to make a weakness look like a strength. On the contrary, common sense presses another truth on us: the more likely it is that people can be saved without missions, the less urgency there is for missions.

So with all three of these questions, there is much at stake. Nevertheless, in the end it is *not* our desire to maintain the urgency of the missionary cause that settles the issue, but: *What do the Scriptures teach?*

My aim in this book is to argue that the teaching of Scripture leads to a positive answer to each of these three questions. I hope to show that in the fullest sense, Jesus is man's only hope for salvation. To do this, I will gather together the biblical texts that relate most directly to the three questions we have posed and make some explanatory comments along the way.

---

21. Crockett and Sigountos, *Through No Fault of Their Own*, 260.

2

Will Anyone Experience Eternal, Conscious Torment under God's Wrath?

Some of the acts of God are extreme—like the size of the universe and the horror of hell. Why is there such a vast universe with so much emptiness? And why is there such a horrible end to a life of suppressing the truth of God? One answer is that finite vastness and horror are designed to make infinite vastness and holiness more clear.

Thus the universe is as large as it is to give suitable meaning to the biblical words, "Heaven, even highest heaven, cannot contain him" (2 Chron. 2:6). If the universe were smaller, the claim that it cannot contain God would tell us less clearly and forcefully how great he is. The larger the universe, the larger our vision of God, who calls it the work of his fingers (Ps. 8:3).

Similarly the horror of hell—its torments and its eternity—is designed to make clear the infinite value of God's glory and the moral horror of idolatry. "Put to death therefore what is earthly in you: sexual immorality, impurity, passion, evil desire, and covetousness, which is idolatry. On account of these the wrath of God is coming" (Col. 3:5–6). There is an idolatry in all our sins—a valuing of something more than God. Hell is God's declaration to the universe that what every sin demeans is of infinite worth.

There Are Mysteries

But our conviction that such a hell exists is not based on our ability to find a suitable explanation for it. It is the other way around. We find our Lord Jesus telling us about hell and convincing us that there is such a reality. And then, because of what he has taught us, we seek in Scripture for an explanation. We do not have to have a satisfactory explanation for everything God tells us is true. There are mysteries: "The secret things belong to the LORD our God, but the things that are revealed belong to us and to our children forever" (Deut. 29:29).

So the main question that faces us concerning hell is: *Does the Bible teach that it exists?* Is there such a reality as eternal conscious torment cut off from the presence of God?[1] To answer this, we will consider the relevant passages of Scripture.

"Shame and Everlasting Contempt"

First, consider one passage from the Old Testament:

> And many of those who sleep in the dust of the earth shall awake, some to everlasting life, and some to shame and *everlasting contempt*.

> Daniel 12:2

It is true that the Hebrew word here for "everlasting" (*olam*) does not always mean endless in a strict temporal sense.[2] But in *this* context, it seems to because it points to a decisive division into joy or misery after death and resurrection. As the *life* after death is everlast-

---

1. For a thorough assessment of the recent departures from historic belief in hell as eternal, conscious torment of the ungodly, I recommend Ajith Fernando, *Crucial Questions about Hell* (Wheaton: Crossway, 1994); Robert A. Peterson, *Hell on Trial: The Case for Eternal Punishment* (Phillipsburg, NJ: P&R, 1995); Carson, *Gagging of God*, 515–36; Larry Dixon, *The Other Side of the Good News: Confronting the Contemporary Challenges to Jesus' Teaching on Hell* (Fearn, UK: Christian Focus, 2003); Robert A. Peterson and Edward William Fudge, *Two Views on Hell: A Biblical and Theological Dialogue* (Downers Grove, IL: InterVarsity, 2000).

2. See the article on *olam* in the *New International Dictionary of Old Testament Theology and Exegesis* (Grand Rapids: Zondervan, 1997), 345–51: "'*olam* is usually used to describe events extended into the distant past or future. Such distant time is clearly relative: it can be time in one's own life (Ps. 77:5 [6]), a life span (Exod. 21:6), or the furthest conceivable time (15:18)." This article includes Daniel 12:2 in the section illustrating the meaning of "unceasingness or perpetuity" (348).

ing, so the *shame and contempt* are everlasting. There is no thought in the Old or the New Testament that after the resurrection divides humanity into *life* and *contempt*, this division will ever be replaced by a new condition.

Moreover, the words used to describe the plight of the lost, "some to *shame* and everlasting *contempt*," (sometimes translated "reproach and everlasting abhorrence") imply an ongoing existence in which this *reproach* and *abhorrence* continues to fall on them. If nonexistence were implied (annihilation), then it would be strange that they were "awakened" from the dust to experience this. The more natural meaning is that they are raised from the dead bodily so that they can be assigned bodily and consciously to their appointed destinies.

"Unquenchable Fire"

Moving to the New Testament, we read of John the Baptist's prediction of the judgment that Jesus would bring in the end.

> His winnowing fork is in his hand, and he will clear his threshing floor and gather his wheat into the barn, but the chaff he will burn with *unquenchable fire*.
>
> Matthew 3:12 (cf. Luke 3:17)

He pictures a decisive separation between the wheat and the chaff. The term "unquenchable fire" implies a fire that will not be extinguished, and therefore a punishment that will not end. If the fire were understood as consuming the chaff so that it ceased to exist, there would seem to be no point in calling it "unquenchable" fire. The natural point is that the fire of punishment never goes out. This understanding is confirmed in Mark 9:43–48:

> And if your hand causes you to sin, cut it off. It is better for you to enter life crippled than with two hands to go to hell, to the *unquenchable fire*. And if your foot causes you to sin, cut it off. It is better for you to enter life lame than with two feet to be thrown into hell. And if your eye causes you to sin, tear it out. It is better for you to enter the kingdom of God with one eye than with two eyes to be thrown into hell, "*where their worm does not die and the fire is not quenched.*"

Here the "unquenchable fire" is clearly hell, and people go there. This is no longer John the Baptist's image of chaff being burned. This is people with feet and hands being "thrown" there. The last line shows that the point is the unending misery of those who go there ("their worm does not die").

Eternal Fire, Destruction, and Punishment

Even though some argue that the fire of God's wrath annihilates the sinner,[3] this is very unlikely. If anni-

---

3. Clark Pinnock of McMaster Divinity College argues that "the 'fire' of God's judgment consumes the lost. . . . God does not raise the wicked in order to torture them consciously forever, but rather to declare his judgment upon the wicked and to condemn them to extinction, which is the second death" (Clark Pinnock, "Fire, Then Nothing," *Christianity Today*, March 20, 1987,

hilation were in view, why would the stress be laid on the fire not ever being quenched and the worm never dying? John Stott struggles to escape this by saying that the worm will not die nor the fire be quenched "until presumably their work of destruction is done."[4] That qualification is not in the text. But the focus on eternal duration is confirmed in Matthew 18:8:

> And if your hand or your foot causes you to sin, cut it off and throw it away. It is better for you to enter life crippled or lame than with two hands or two feet to be thrown into the *eternal fire.*

Here the fire is not only unquenchable, but more explicitly, "eternal." That this fire is not merely a purifying fire of the age to come (as some take "eternal" [*aiōnion*] to mean) will be shown in the subsequent sayings of Jesus.

Sometimes the case is made that the term "destroy" in regard to final judgment means "annihilate." But this is not at all obvious or necessary. For example, Jesus says,

> And do not fear those who kill the body but cannot kill the soul. Rather fear him who can *destroy* both soul and body in hell.

> Matthew 10:28 (cf. Luke 12:4–5)

---

49). See also Clark H. Pinnock, "The Conditional View," in *Four Views on Hell*, ed. William Crockett (Grand Rapids: Zondervan, 1996), 135–66.

4. John Stott, quoted in Edwards, *Evangelical Essentials*, 317.

The "destruction" referred to here is decisive and final, but it does not have to mean "obliterate" or "annihilate." The word *apolumi* frequently means "ruin" or "lose" or "perish" or "get rid of" (Matt. 8:25; 9:17; 10:6; 12:14). It does not imply annihilate. It is eternal ruin (see 2 Thess. 1:9 on pages 42–43).

The contrast between eternal life and eternal punishment in the teaching of Jesus is significant. In the description of the final judgment as a division between sheep and goats, the king divides the people and says, "Depart from me, you cursed, into the *eternal fire* prepared for the devil and his angels" (Matt. 25:41). Then Jesus gives his interpretation: "And these will go away into *eternal punishment*, but the righteous into eternal life" (Matt. 25:46).

Here the eternal fire is explicitly called eternal *punishment*. And its opposite is eternal *life*. It does not honor the full import of "eternal life" to say that it only refers to a quality of life without the connotation of everlasting.[5] Scot McKnight devotes extensive treatment to Matthew 25:46 in view of the efforts of many to see the eternal consequence of unrighteousness as annihilation. His conclusion is solid:

> The terms for *eternal* in Matthew 25:46 pertain to the final age, and a distinguishing feature of the final age, in contrast to this age, is that it is eternal, endless, and temporally unlimited. It follows then that the most probable meaning of Matthew 25:46

5. Scot McKnight, "Eternal Consequences or Eternal Consciousness," in Crockett and Sigountos, *Through No Fault of Their Own*, 157.

is that just as life with God is temporally unlimited for the righteous, so punishment for sin and rejection of Christ is also temporally unlimited. . . . [T]he final state of the wicked is conscious, eternal torment.[6]

"For the Devil and His Angels"

Not only that, but when you compare this text to Revelation 20:10, the case for conscious eternal torment is strengthened. Here in Matthew 25:41, the "goats" are sentenced to "eternal fire prepared *for the devil and his angels.*" This is precisely what is described in Revelation 20:10, namely, the final destiny of the devil. "The devil who had deceived them was thrown into the lake of fire and sulfur where the beast and the false prophet were, and they will be tormented *day and night forever and ever*" (Rev. 20:10). The condition is clearly one of conscious torment (see pages 45–46).

Better Not to Have Been Born

One of the most striking statements Jesus ever made about the existence of a human being is the statement that it would have been better for Judas if he had never existed.

6. Ibid.

The Son of Man goes as it is written of him, but woe to that man by whom the Son of Man is betrayed! *It would have been better for that man if he had not been born.*

Matthew 26:24

If Judas were destined for glory eventually (as in universalism), or even destined for extinction (as in annihilationism), it is difficult to imagine why it would have been better for him not to have been born. If his life had been filled with misery, and there were no pleasures in his life, and this life was to be followed by extinction, then never coming into existence might make sense. But is that what Jesus is saying about Judas—that in this life there was not enough pleasure to make it worthwhile for him to have existed? I cannot even imagine Jesus thinking that way.

No, it seems much more likely that Jesus means that Judas's future is so terrible that he will regret having come into existence. When Jesus calls Judas the "son of destruction" (John 17:12), he means that by his nature as deceiver and thief and betrayer he was headed for destruction. And this word "destruction" (*apoleias*) is the noun form of the verb "destroy" (*apolesai*) in Matthew 10:28, "Fear him who can *destroy* both soul and body in hell." This means that Jesus saw Judas as hell-bent by his nature. That is why it would have been better for him not to have existed.

A Sin That Will Never Be Forgiven

As if in response to the claim by George MacDonald and others that eventually all sins will be forgiven and all beings will be reformed and brought to glory, Jesus says that there is a kind of sin that will never be forgiven.

> Whoever speaks a word against the Son of Man will be forgiven; but whoever speaks against the Holy Spirit will not be forgiven, either in this age *or in the age to come.*
>
> Matthew 12:32

This rules out the idea that after a time of suffering in hell, sinners will then be reformed and forgiven and admitted to the glorious presence of God. Jesus says that there will be no forgiveness in the age to come for the unforgivable sin, and so in Mark, Jesus calls it an *eternal* sin, that is, a sin which will not be forgiven for eternity. "Whoever blasphemes against the Holy Spirit never has forgiveness, but is guilty of an *eternal sin*" (Mark 3:29). This does not disprove annihilationism. But it does disprove the kind of universalism that says everyone will someday be forgiven and reformed and saved.

"I Am in Anguish in This Flame"

But neither annihilationism nor universalism will fit with what Jesus says about the rich man who refused to care for the poor man Lazarus at his gate. The rich man died and went to the place of "torment" (Luke 16:23), and Lazarus died and went to "Abraham's side" (Luke 16:22). Jesus says that the rich man "called out, 'Father Abraham, have mercy on me, and send Lazarus to dip the end of his finger in water and cool my tongue, for *I am in anguish in this flame*'" (Luke 16:24).

Abraham's response defines the relationship between heaven and hell:

> [Lazarus] is comforted here, and you are in anguish. And besides all this, between us and you a great chasm has been fixed, in order that those who would pass from here to you may not be able, and *none may cross from there to us.*
>
> Luke 16:25–26

The point is that the suffering there cannot be escaped. There is no way out. This is the terrible picture that Jesus paints for us again and again in the Gospels. No one is more full or fearsome in describing the horrors or the endlessness of hell than Jesus. This is not a teaching created by the apostles or the early church. It was given to us by the Lord. The most loving man that ever walked the earth gave the strongest and fullest description of hell.

Surely we are to learn from this that an essential part of his loving mission to rescue sinners included then, and should include now, the clear conviction and warning that there is an eternal misery awaiting everyone who does not obey him. "Whoever believes in the Son has eternal life; whoever does not obey the

Son shall not see life, but *the wrath of God remains on him*" (John 3:36).

Flaming Fire and Final Destruction

When we turn now to the apostles' teaching, we find the warnings of Jesus affirmed. In Romans 2:6–8 Paul says,

> [God] will render to each one according to his works: to those who by patience in well-doing seek for glory and honor and immortality, he will give *eternal* life; but for those who are self-seeking and do not obey the truth, but obey unrighteousness, there will be *wrath and fury*.

This text is significant because "wrath and fury" are the alternative to "eternal life." This seems to imply that the wrath and fury are experienced instead of life "eternally"—forever. But it could mean, without any other clues, that the wrath and fury expend themselves quickly and annihilate the unrighteous, or that they eventually burn the impurity out of the unrighteous and lead them to glory.

But there are other clues that don't encourage us to think that way. For example, in 2 Thessalonians 1:7–10, Paul describes the coming of Christ in judgment:

> The Lord Jesus [will be] revealed from heaven with his mighty angels in flaming fire, inflicting vengeance on those who do not know God and on those who do

not obey the gospel of our Lord Jesus. *They will suffer the punishment of eternal destruction,* away from the presence of the Lord and from the glory of his might, when he comes on that day to be glorified in his saints, and to be marveled at among all who have believed, because our testimony to you was believed.

The word here for "destruction" (*olethros*) means "ruin," not "obliteration." For example, it is used in 1 Corinthians 5:5, where Paul says of the man who is handed over in church discipline to Satan: "You are to deliver this man to Satan for the *destruction/ruin* [*olethron*] of the flesh, so that his spirit may be saved in the day of the Lord." This does not mean that his flesh is obliterated, but that the man experiences enough ruin in his flesh that he will repent and be restored to the Lord and the church.

Therefore, when Paul speaks of unbelievers suffering "the punishment of eternal destruction," he is very likely referring to the kind of ongoing misery that they experience in hell from the just sentence of the "one who can destroy both soul and body in hell" (Matt. 10:28).

"Eternal Judgment"

If we consider the teaching of the book of Hebrews, we meet the phrase "eternal judgment."

Let us leave the elementary doctrine of Christ and go on to maturity, not laying again a foundation of repentance from dead works and of faith toward God, and of instruction about washings, the laying on of hands, the resurrection of the dead, and *eternal judgment*.

Hebrews 6:1–2

One of the rudimentary teachings of the church was that there would be an eternal judgment. The author later says in Hebrews 9:27–28, "Just as it is appointed for man to die once, and after that comes *judgment*, so Christ, having been offered once to bear the sins of many, will appear a second time, not to deal with sin but to save those who are eagerly waiting for him." But here in chapter 6, he calls this judgment an "eternal judgment." What does this mean?

It probably does not mean that the act of judging, as in a courtroom, goes on forever, but that the outcomes of the judgment are eternal. John Owen, in his classic commentary, says, "This judgment is called 'eternal' . . . because in it and by it an *unchangeable determination* of all men's estate and condition is made for eternity—the judgment which disposeth of men unalterably into their eternal estate, whether of blessedness or of misery."[7]

"The Smoke of Their Torment Goes Up for Ever and Ever"

Finally, we turn to the book of Revelation, where the apostle John gives us the strongest words in the New

7. John Owen, *An Exposition of the Epistle to the Hebrews* (Edinburgh: Banner of Truth Trust, 1991), 5:47 (emphasis added).

Testament for the eternal duration of the torments of hell. An angel says with a loud voice,

> "If anyone worships the beast and its image and receives a mark on his forehead or on his hand, he also will drink the wine of God's wrath, poured full strength into the cup of his anger, and he will be tormented with fire and sulfur in the presence of the holy angels and in the presence of the Lamb. And *the smoke of their torment goes up forever and ever, and they have no rest, day or night*, these worshipers of the beast and its image, and whoever receives the mark of its name."
>
> Here is a call for the endurance of the saints.

Revelation 14:9–12

We have no reason to think that these unbelievers are in some special class from all the others in Scripture. Therefore, what it says about them is true for all: "*the smoke of their torment goes up forever and ever, and they have no rest, day or night.*" There is no stronger Greek expression for eternity than the one rendered here "forever and ever." Literally it could read, "unto ages of ages" (*eis aiōnas aiōnōn*).

The phrase occurs, with the articles (*eis tous aiōnas tōn aiōnōn*), nineteen times in the New Testament. In relation to hell, it occurs in Revelation 19:3, "Once more they cried, 'Hallelujah! The smoke from her goes up *forever and ever,*'" and in Revelation 20:10, "And the devil who had deceived them was thrown into the lake of fire and sulfur where the beast and the false prophet were, and they will be tormented *day and night forever and ever.*"

The connection between Revelation 14:11 and Revelation 20:10 is significant because the reality of conscious eternal "torment" is underlined. Both texts refer to torment, not extinction. G. K. Beale remarks on Revelation 14:11,

> Two considerations support the view that eternal, ongoing punishment is spoken of here. First, the parallel in 20:10 refers to the devil, beast, and false prophet undergoing the judgment in "the lake of fire and brimstone," where "they will be tormented day and night forever and ever." This does not say that their existence will be abolished forever but that they will suffer torment forever. . . . The ungodly suffer the same fate as their three Satanic leaders who represent them. . . . Furthermore 22:14–15 implies that the existence of the wicked is coterminous with the eternal blessedness of the righteous.
>
> Second, the word βασανισμός [*basanismos*] ("torment") in Rev. 14:11 is used nowhere in Revelation or biblical literature in the sense of annihilation of personal existence. Without exception, Revelation uses it of conscious suffering on the part of people (9:5; 11:10; 12:2; 18:7, 10, 15; 20:10).[8]

No Escape from the Texts

John Stott struggles in vain to escape the clear intent of the eternal torments of the lake of fire. He says that

8. G. K. Beale, *The Book of Revelation* (Grand Rapids: Eerdmans, 1999), 762.

Revelation 20:10 refers to the beast and false prophet who "are not individual people but symbols of the world in its varied hostility to God. In the nature of the case they cannot experience pain."[9]

But Stott fails to mention Revelation 20:15 where it says that "if anyone's name [not just the beast and false prophet] was not found written in the book of life, he was thrown into the lake of fire." Similarly, Revelation 21:8 says that it is *individual sinners* whose "portion will be in the lake that burns with fire and sulfur, which is the second death." And the torment that lasts "forever and ever" in Revelation 14:11 is precisely the torment of people "with fire and sulfur"—that is, the torment of "the lake that burns with fire and sulfur" (21:8).

In other words, the "lake of fire" is in view not only, as Stott suggests, when the beast and false prophet and death and Hades (20:13–14) are cast into it, but also when individual unbelievers are finally condemned and thrown in as well (14:10–11; 20:15; 21:8), and that shows decisively that individual unbelieving persons will experience eternal, conscious torment.[10]

---

9. John Stott, quoted in Edwards, *Evangelical Essentials*, 318.

10. John Stott was gracious enough to correspond with me personally about this issue of the eternal fate of the lost. To be fair to one I count a brother and a theological and pastoral mentor for more than thirty years, I want to give his perspective on what I have written from a personal letter dated March 1, 1993. I have tried to take his criticisms into account in this edition. He writes:

I cannot honestly say that I think you have done justice to what I have written in *Evangelical Essentials*. . . . For example, I do strongly affirm all the "eternal" and "unquenchable" verses which you quote, and do believe in

Conclusion

Hell is a dreadful reality. To speak of it lightly proves we do not grasp its horror. I know of no one who has overstated the terrors of hell. We can scarcely surpass the horrid images Jesus used. We are meant to shudder.

Why? Because the infinite horrors of hell are intended by God to be a vivid demonstration of the infinite value of his glory which sinners have belittled. The biblical assumption of the justice of hell[11] is the

---

"eternal punishment." It is not the eternity, but the nature, of the punishment which is under discussion. You do not make this clear.

I also believe in torment in the interim state (as the Lazarus story shows), and that there will be terrible "weeping and gnashing of teeth" when the lost learn their fate. I think I believe as strongly as you do that "it is a fearful thing to fall into the hands of the living God."

What troubles me is the way you tend to quote proof texts as knockdown arguments, when they are capable of alternative interpretations. I just find you over-dogmatic, as I wrote in my earlier letter, leaving no room for the humble agnosticism which allows that God has not revealed everything as plainly as you make out.

I mentioned to Dr. Stott in an earlier letter that my less than positive attitude toward agnosticism and tentativity is probably influenced by the sea of relativism that I am trying to navigate, both inside and outside the church. I do not want to communicate an unwillingness to learn or to change as new light on the Scripture emerges. But my diagnosis of the sickness of our times inclines me less toward "humble agnosticism" and more toward (I hope) "humble affirmation." Whether I have moved from warranted and well-grounded firmness of conviction into unwarranted and poorly argued dogmatism, I leave for others to judge.

11. One person who has wrestled with the justice of hell and moved toward a very unusual position on annihilationism and the traditional view of conscious, eternal misery is Greg Boyd, who represents so-called Open Theism. In his *Satan and the Problem of Evil* (Downers Grove, IL: InterVarsity, 2001), Boyd attempts to handle the texts used to argue for the eternal,

clearest testimony to the infiniteness of the sin of failing to glorify God. All of us have failed. All the

conscious torment of hell and the texts used to argue for annihilationism by "affirming both views as essentially correct" (336).

On the one hand, he says, "When all the biblical evidence is viewed together, it must be admitted that the case for annihilationism is quite compelling" (336). But he sees some texts on the other side that do not fit the simple annihilationist view (he mentions Rev. 14:10; 20:10; Matt. 25:34, 41; 2 Thess. 1:6–9 [336]).

He asks, "Where does this leave us? For my part, it leaves me in a conundrum. I do not believe that either the traditional position or the annihilationists' position adequately accounts for all the biblical evidence cited in support of the opposing side's position. Yet I do not believe that Scripture can contradict itself (John 10:35). This raises the question: Is there a logically consistent way of affirming both views as essentially correct?" (336–37).

His answer is yes: "I will attempt to move beyond the impasse of the traditional and annihilationist understandings of eternal punishment and construct a model of hell that allows us to affirm the essence of both perspectives" (339). As paradoxical as it sounds, he attempts to show that "hell is the eternal suffering of agents who have been annihilated" (356).

He states a crucial premise: "There can be no shared reality between those who say yes to God and those who say no, just as there can be no shared reality between the actuality that God affirms and the possibilities that God negates" (347). Here is the conclusion that follows: "Love is about relationships, and relationships are about sharing reality. Hence, when in the eschaton reality is exhaustively defined by God's love, the 'reality' of any agent who opposes love cannot be shared by anyone else and thus cannot be real to anyone else. It is experienced as real *from the inside* of the one who sustains it by his or her active willing it. But to all who participate in reality—that is, who are open to God and to each other through the medium of God's love—it is nothing. It is eternally willed nothingness" (350). "Hell is real only from the inside" (348).

Thus "we are able to affirm that in one sense the inhabitants of hell are annihilated, though they suffer eternally. From the perspective of all who share reality in the eschaton, the damned are no more (Obad. 16). They exist only as utter negation.... They continue to experience torment, but it is a torment of their own pathetic choosing in an illusory reality of their own damned imagining" (350). "As Scripture says, they are extinct, reduced to ashes, forever forgotten.... But we may also accept the scriptural teaching regarding nations have failed. Therefore, the weight of infinite guilt rests on every human head because of our failure to delight in God more than we delight in our own self-sufficiency.

The vision of God in Scripture is of a majestic and sovereign God who does all things to magnify the greatness of his glory for the everlasting enjoyment of his people. And the view of man in Scripture is that man suppresses this truth and finds more joy in his own glory than he does in God's (see Rom. 1:18–32).

When Clark Pinnock[12] and John Stott[13] repeat the centuries-old objection that an *eternal* punishment is disproportionate to a *finite* life of sinning, they disregard the essential thing that Jonathan Edwards saw so clearly. The essential thing is that degrees of blameworthiness come not from how *long* you offend dignity, but from *how high* the dignity is that you offend.

---

the eternity of the torment of the reprobate. . . . From the inside of the rebel experience, the nothingness that they have willed is experienced as a something. To all others, it is nothing" (352–53).

I am not persuaded that Boyd's complex and paradoxical "model" can survive close scrutiny. An extended critique of this view exceeds the bounds of this book, but I have written a partial response titled "Greg Boyd on the 'The Eternal Suffering of Agents Who Have Been Annihilated,'" Desiring God website, March 6, 2002, http://www.desiringgod.org/ResourceLibrary/TasteAndSee/ByDate/2002/1197.

12. Clark Pinnock says, "It just does not make sense to say that a God of love will torture people forever for sins done in the context of a finite life" (Pinnock and Brown, *Theological Crossfire*, 226).

13. John Stott says, "Would there not be serious disproportion between sins consciously committed in time and torment consciously experienced throughout eternity?" (quoted in Edwards, *Evangelical Essentials*, 318).

The crime of one being's despising, and casting contempt on another, is proportionably more or less heinous as he was under greater or lesser obligations to honor him: the fault of disobeying another, is greater or less, as anyone is under greater or lesser obligations to obey him. And therefore if there be any being, that we are under infinite obligations to love, and honor, and obey, the contrary towards him must be infinitely faulty.

Our obligation to love, honor, and obey any being, is in proportion to his loveliness, honorableness, and authority. . . . But God is a being infinitely lovely, because he hath infinite excellency and beauty. . . .

So that sin against God being a violation of infinite obligations, must be a crime infinitely heinous; and so deserving of infinite punishment. . . . The eternity of the punishment of ungodly men renders it infinite; and it renders it no more than infinite; and therefore renders no more than proportionable to the heinousness of what they are guilty of.[14]

One key difference between Edwards and our contemporary spokesmen who abandon the historic biblical view of hell is that Edwards was radically committed to deriving his views of God's justice and love *from*

14. Jonathan Edwards, "The Justice of God in the Damnation of Sinners," in *Sermons and Discourses 1734–1738*, vol. 19, *The Works of Jonathan Edwards* (New Haven: Yale University Press, 2001), 342–43. For expositions of Edwards's view on hell, see John Gerstner, *Jonathan Edwards on Heaven and Hell* (Grand Rapids: Baker, 1980), and Chris Morgan, *Hell and Jonathan Edwards: Toward a God-Centered Theology of Hell* (Fearn, UK: Christian Focus, 2003).

God. But more and more, it seems, contemporary evangelicals are submitting to what "makes sense" to their own moral sentiments.[15] This will not strengthen the church or its mission. What is needed is a radical commitment to the supremacy of God in determining what is real and what is not.

15. See Pinnock's quotes in note 12 of chapter 1 and note 12 of chapter 2, and Stott's quotes in note 13 of chapter 1 and note 13 of chapter 2 above. Another thing that seems to have been overlooked is that in hell the sins of the unrepentant go on forever and ever. People do not become righteous in hell. They are given over to the corruption of their nature so that they continue rebelling and deserving eternal punishment eternally.

3

Is the Work of Jesus Necessary for Salvation?

The second question we must ask as part of our enquiry is whether Christ's work of atonement is necessary for the salvation of whoever is saved. Are there people who can be saved another way than by the efficacy of Christ's work? Are other religions, and the provisions they offer, sufficient for bringing people to eternal happiness with God?

The biblical texts discussed below lead us to believe that Christ's atonement is indeed necessary for the salvation of everyone who is saved. There is no salvation apart from what Jesus achieved in his death and resurrection.

The Act of Adam and the Act of Christ

The universal necessity of Christ's redeeming work is set forth clearly in Romans 5 where the act of Christ in salvation is correlated with the act of Adam in universal condemnation.

> If, because of one man's trespass, death reigned through that one man, much more will those who receive the abundance of grace and the free gift of righteousness reign in life through the one man Jesus Christ.
>
> Therefore, as one man's trespass led to condemnation for all men, so one man's act of righteousness leads to justification and life for all men. For as by one man's disobedience many were made sinners, so by the one man's obedience many will be made righteous.
>
> Romans 5:17–19

The crucial point here is *the universality of the work of Christ* in regard to all humanity. It is not done in a corner with reference merely to Jews. The work of Christ, the second Adam, corresponds to the work of the first Adam. As the sin of Adam leads to condemnation for all humanity that are united to him as their head, so the obedience of Christ leads to righteousness for all humanity that are united to him as their head—"those who receive the abundance of grace" (v. 17).

The work of Christ in the obedience of the cross is pictured as the divine answer to the plight of the whole human race. It is not presented as one way among many to remedy the condemnation that happened to all humans through Adam. The obedience of one man, Christ Jesus, is God's answer to the fallenness of the whole human race.

We see this again in 1 Corinthians 15:21–23:

For as by a man came death, by a man has come also the resurrection of the dead. For as in Adam all die, so also in Christ shall all be made alive. But each in his own order: Christ the firstfruits, then at his coming those who belong to Christ.

In this text, Jesus's resurrection is made the answer to the universal human misery of death. Adam is the head of the old humanity marked by death. Jesus is the head of the new humanity marked by resurrection. The members of this new humanity are "those who belong to Christ" (v. 23).[1] Christ is not a tribal deity relating merely to the woes of one group. He is given

---

1. Note that it would be an incorrect, superficial reading of this text, as well as of Romans 5:17–19, to assume that it is teaching universalism in the sense that all human beings will be saved. The "all" who are acquitted in Romans 5 are defined in Romans 5:17 as "those who receive the abundance of grace." And the "all" who are made alive in 1 Corinthians 15:22 are defined as "those who belong to Christ." The term "justification and life for all men" in Romans 5:18 does not mean that every human being who is in Adam will also be justified so that no one will perish and that there is no such thing as eternal punishment for anyone. I say this for several reasons.

First, verse 17 speaks of "receiving" the gift of righteousness as though some do and some do not: "For if, because of one man's trespass, death reigned through that one man, much more will *those who receive the abundance of grace and the free gift of righteousness* reign in life through the one man Jesus Christ." That does not sound like everybody does receive it.

Second, "justification and life for all men" in Romans 5:18 does not mean all humans are justified because Paul teaches in this very book that there is eternal punishment and that all humans are not justified. For example, in Romans 2:5 he says, "But because of your hard and impenitent heart you are storing up wrath for yourself on the day of wrath when God's righteous judgment will be revealed," and then in verses 7 and 8, he contrasts this wrath with "eternal life" and so shows that it is eternal wrath, not temporary wrath. So there will be some who are not justified but come under the wrath of God forever and others who have eternal life.

as God's answer to the universal problem of death. Those who attain to the resurrection of the dead attain it in Christ.

One Mediator between God and Man

This universal work of Christ in correlation with the fall of the whole human race also corresponds to the way Paul talks about Christ as the mediator of salvation. He says, "There is one God, and there is one mediator between God and men, the man Christ Jesus, who gave himself a ransom for all (1 Tim. 2:5–6).

This is not spoken with any one group of people in mind but with humanity in mind: "one mediator between God and men." Not God and Jews, or God and any other ethnic or religious group. The problem between God and humanity is one, and God sent one mediator to deal with it.

The Lamb Purchases a People from All Nations

The whole book of Revelation pictures Jesus as the King of kings and Lord of lords (17:14; 19:16)—the universal

---

Third, "justification and life for all men" in Romans 5:18 does not mean all humans are justified because in all of Romans up until now justification is not automatic as if every human receives it, but it is "by faith." Romans 5:1: "Therefore, since we have been *justified by faith* . . ."; Romans 3:28: "For we hold that one is *justified by faith* apart from works of the law." Further, a universalistic reading of Paul's "all" statements renders Paul's intense grief (Rom. 9:3)—to the point of wishing he could perish, if possible, on their behalf—unintelligible.

ruler over all peoples and powers. Though he is God and Lord before his incarnation, there is a sense in which Christ ascended to his universal redeeming role through his suffering, by which he became a universal Savior.

> Worthy are you to take the scroll
>   and to open its seals,
> for you were slain, and by your blood you
>   ransomed people for God
>   from every tribe and language and
>   people and nation,
> and you have made them a kingdom and
>   priests to our God,
>   and they shall reign on the earth.
>
> Revelation 5:9–10

These verses show that Jesus purchased a people for himself from *all the tribes and languages of the world.* God did not plan multiple saviors for multiple peoples. He planned one Savior for all peoples. His atonement is the means in every culture by which men and women become part of his kingdom.

Christ Died to Gather the Children from All the World

John had said the same thing in his Gospel by recording the prophecy of Caiaphas that "Jesus would die for the nation, and not for the nation only, but also to gather into one the children of God who are scattered abroad" (John 11:51–52). The point of that prophecy is that the saving work of Jesus is not meant by God to be limited to one people but is the means by which God would save his elect from all the peoples of the world.

Perhaps Peter said it more clearly than anyone in his sermon in Jerusalem in Acts 4. "And there is salvation in no one else, for there is no other name under heaven given among men by which we must be saved" (Acts 4:12). The work of Christ is not mentioned here explicitly, but the universality of his name as the only way to salvation would imply that whatever he did to win salvation for his people (namely, shed his blood; Acts 20:28) has universal significance. There are no other ways that a person in any other religion can be saved. If anyone would be saved, he must be saved by the name of Jesus.

One Remedy for Universal Unrighteousness: Justification in Jesus

Finally, we should remember that the very structure of the book of Romans, not just chapter 5, which we looked at earlier, is built to show the universality of sin and the work of Christ as the answer to that universal problem. Paul concludes from the first two chapters, "We have already charged that all, both Jews and Greeks, are under sin, as it is written: 'None is righteous, no, not one'" (Rom. 3:9–10). That is what the book is written to deal with. None is righteous. Which means if there is no way for the unrighteous to be justified, no one will be saved anywhere in the world.

He makes the universality of the problem clear in Romans 3:19: "Now we know that whatever the law says it speaks to those who are under the law, so *that every mouth may be stopped, and the whole world may be held accountable to God.*" The law's function with Israel was universal in scope. "The whole world" has become accountable to God for its sin.

What is the remedy? The next verse connects the word of God in Christ to the universality of the need:

> But now the righteousness of God has been manifested apart from the law, although the Law and the Prophets bear witness to it—the righteousness of God through faith in Jesus Christ for all who believe. For there is no distinction: for all have sinned and fall short of the glory of God, and are justified by his grace as a gift, through the redemption that is in Christ Jesus.
>
> Romans 3:21–24

It is crystal clear that "the redemption that is in Christ Jesus" is given by God as the solution for the universal problem of sin. The thought that there are other saviors or other ways of getting right with God besides what is presented in these verses is an imagination of man, not a revelation of God.

Conclusion

In answer to our second question, the New Testament makes clear that the atoning work of Christ is not merely for Jews or merely for any one nation or tribe or language. It is the one and only way for anyone to get right with God. The problem of sin is universal, cutting people off from God. The solution to that problem is the atoning death of the Son of God offered once for all. This is the very foundation of missions. Since the work of Christ is the only basis for salvation,[2] it must be announced to all the nations, as the resurrected Jesus himself says to his disciples in Luke 24:46–47:

> Thus it is written, that the Christ should suffer and on the third day rise from the dead, and that repentance and forgiveness of sins should be proclaimed in his name to all nations, beginning from Jerusalem.

2. For further study of the significance of Christ's death, consider the following texts: Mark 10:45; Matthew 26:28; John 1:29; 6:51; Romans 4:25–5:1; 5:6, 8–10; 1 Corinthians 15:3; 2 Corinthians 5:18–21; Galatians 1:4; 4:4; Ephesians 1:7; 2:1–5, 13, 16, 18; 5:2, 25; Colossians 1:20; 1 Thessalonians 5:9; Titus 2:14; 1 Timothy 4:10; Hebrews 1:3; 9:12, 22, 26; 10:14; 12:24; 13:12; 1 Peter 1:19; 2:24; 3:18; 1 John 2:2; Revelation 1:5.

4

Is Conscious Faith in Jesus Necessary for Salvation?

Part One: The Mystery of Christ and the Times of Ignorance

The question that concerns us here is whether some people are awakened by the Holy Spirit and saved by grace through faith in a merciful Creator even though they never hear of Jesus in this life. In other words, are there devout people in other religions who humbly rely on the grace of the God whom they know through nature (Rom. 1:19–21), and thus receive eternal salvation?[1]

1. Clark Pinnock embraces the idea that people from other religions will be saved without knowing Christ. "We do not need to think of the church as the ark

Something of immense historical significance happened with the coming of the Son of God into the

_____

of salvation, leaving everyone else in hell; we can rather think of it as the chosen witness to the fullness of salvation that has come into the world through Jesus" (Clark H. Pinnock, "Acts 4:12—No Other Name Under Heaven," in Crockett and Sigountos, *Through No Fault of Their Own,* 113). See also Clark H. Pinnock, *A Wideness in God's Mercy: The Finality of Jesus Christ in a World of Religions* (Grand Rapids: Zondervan, 1992), and Clark H. Pinnock, "An Inclusivist View," in *Four Views on Salvation in a Pluralistic Age,* ed. Dennis L. Okholm and Timothy R. Phillips (Grand Rapids: Zondervan, 1995), 95–123.

Pinnock is following others with similar views: Charles Kraft, *Christianity in Culture* (Maryknoll, NY: Orbis, 1979), 253–57; James N. D. Anderson, *Christianity and World Religions* (Downers Grove, IL: InterVarsity, 1984), chap. 5; John E. Sanders, "Is Belief in Christ Necessary for Salvation?" *Evangelical Quarterly* 60 (1988): 241–59; and John Sanders, *No Other Name: An Investigation into the Destiny of the Unevangelized* (Grand Rapids: Eerdmans, 1992). Perhaps the best defense of the inclusivist position by someone within the Reformed camp would be Terrance L. Tiessen, *Who Can Be Saved? Reassessing Salvation in Christ and World Religions* (Downers Grove, IL: InterVarsity, 2004). He calls his position *accessibilism.* See also Neal Punt, *A Theology of Inclusivism* (Allendale, MI: Northland Books, 2008).

For a short survey of representatives on both sides of the question, see Malcolm J. McVeigh, "The Fate of Those Who've Never Heard? It Depends," *Evangelical Missions Quarterly* 21, no. 4 (October 1985): 370–79. For books with multiple views represented, see *What about Those Who Have Never Heard? Three Views on the Destiny of the Unevangelized,* ed. John Sanders (Grand Rapids: Zondervan, 1995); and Okholm and Phillips, *Four Views on Salvation in a Pluralistic Age.* For a critique of inclusivism, see Christopher W. Morgan and Robert A. Peterson, eds., *Faith Comes by Hearing: A Response to Inclusivism* (Downers Grove, IL: InterVarsity, 2007); Carson, *Gagging of God,* 279–314; Dick Dowsett, *God, That's Not Fair!* (Sevenoaks, UK: OMF Books, 1982); Ronald H. Nash, *Is Jesus the Only Savior?* (Grand Rapids: Zondervan, 1994); Ramesh Richard, *The Population of Heaven* (Chicago: Moody, 1994); Paul R. House and Gregory A. Thornbury, eds., *Who Will Be Saved? Defending the Biblical Understanding of God, Salvation, and Evangelism* (Wheaton: Crossway, 2000), 111–60; the contributions of R. Douglas Geivett and W. Gary Phillips in Okholm and Phillips, *Four Views on Salvation in a Pluralistic Age;* Daniel Strange, *The Possibility of Salvation among the Unevangelized: An Analysis of Inclusivism in Recent Evangelical Theology* (Carlisle: Paternoster, 2003);

world. So great was the significance of this event that the focus of saving faith was, from that time on, made to center on Jesus Christ alone. So fully does Christ sum up all the revelation of God and all the hopes of God's people that it would henceforth be a dishonor to him should saving faith repose on anyone but him.[2]

Before his coming, a grand "mystery" was kept secret for ages. With the uncovering of this mystery, the "times of ignorance" (Acts 17:30)[3] ended, and the call to repentance now sounds forth with a new specificity: Jesus Christ has been appointed Judge of all peoples

---

and Harold A. Netland, "One Lord and Savior for All? Jesus Christ and Religious Diversity," The Gospel Coalition Christ on Campus Initiative, http://thegospelcoalition.org/publications/cci.

2. There is a continuity between God's path to salvation in the Old Testament times and the path through faith in Jesus during the New Testament times. Even before Christ, people were not saved apart from special revelation given by God. See Ajith Fernando, The Christian's Attitude toward World Religions (Wheaton: Tyndale, 1987), 136–39. See also Ajith Fernando, Sharing the Truth in Love: How to Relate to People of Other Faiths (Grand Rapids: Discovery House Publishers, 2001), 224–33.

It is not as though general revelation through nature was effective in producing faith before Christ but ceased to be effective after Christ. According to Romans 1:18–23, general revelation through nature has always been sufficient to make people accountable to glorify and thank God, but not efficient to bring them to the point of actually glorifying Christ in a saving way. The reason given is that people in their natural condition suppress the truth. See note 6 of chapter 4 and note 8 of chapter 6. Thus, special revelation has always been the path to salvation, and this special revelation was centered in Israel, the promise of a Redeemer, and the foreshadowings of this salvation in the sacrificial system of the Old Testament. Jesus is now the climax and fulfillment of that special revelation so that saving faith, which was always focused on God's saving work, is now focused on him.

3. See below in the text for an exposition of this phrase.

by virtue of his resurrection from the dead. All appeals for mercy and acquittal must now come through him, and him alone. We turn now to the biblical texts that lay this truth open for us.

"The Mystery of Christ"

Paul writes to the Ephesians about how the nations (with all their varied religions) are brought into the stream of salvation "through the gospel." This is "the mystery of Christ" which is now revealed.

> When you read this, you can perceive my insight into *the mystery of Christ*, which was not made known to the sons of men in other generations as it has now been revealed to his holy apostles and prophets by the Spirit. This *mystery* is that the Gentiles are fellow heirs, members of the same body, and partakers of the promise in Christ Jesus *through the gospel.*
>
> Of this gospel I was made a minister according to the gift of God's grace, which was given me by the working of his power. To me, though I am the very least of all the saints, this grace was given, to preach to the Gentiles the unsearchable riches of Christ, and to bring to light for everyone what is the plan of the mystery hidden for ages in God who created all things, so that through the church the manifold wisdom of God might now be made known to the rulers and authorities in the heavenly places.
>
> Ephesians 3:4–10

There was a truth that was not fully and clearly revealed before the coming of Christ. This truth, now revealed, is called "the mystery of Christ." It is the truth that *people from all the nations of the world are full and complete partners with the chosen people of God* (Eph. 3:6). It is called "the mystery of Christ" because it is coming true "through the gospel" (Eph. 3:6) which is about Christ.

Therefore, the gospel is not the revelation that the nations *already* belong to God. The gospel is the instrument for bringing the nations into this equal status of salvation. The mystery of Christ (drawing the nations into the inheritance of Abraham) is happening through the preaching of the gospel. Paul sees his own apostolic vocation as the means God is graciously using to declare the riches of the Messiah to the nations (Eph. 3:8).

So a massive change has occurred in redemptive history. Before the coming of Christ, a truth was not fully revealed—namely, that the nations may enter with equal standing into the household of God (Eph. 2:19). The time was not "full" for this revelation because Christ had not been revealed from heaven. The glory and honor of uniting all the peoples was being reserved for him in his saving work (Eph. 1:9–10). It is fitting then that the nations be gathered in only through the preaching of the message of Christ, whose cross is the peace that creates the worldwide church (Eph. 2:11–21).

Why There Was No Full-Blown Mission to the Nations before the Incarnation

In other words, there is a profound theological reason why salvation did not spread to the nations before the incarnation of the Son of God. The reason is that it would not have been clear that the nations were gathering for the glory of Christ. God means for his Son to be the center of worship as the nations receive the word of reconciliation. For this reason also we will see further on that the preaching of Christ is the means appointed by God for the ingathering of the nations.

Consider a very complex sentence from the book of Romans. If we patiently examine its parts and notice how they relate to each other (hence the detailed verse numbering), the crucial meaning for our question will appear.

> [25a]Now to him who is able to strengthen you [25b]according to my gospel and the preaching of Jesus Christ, [25c]according to the revelation of the mystery that was kept secret for long ages [26a]but has now been disclosed [26b]and through the prophetic writings has been made known to all nations [26c]according to the command of the eternal God, [26d]to bring about the obedience of faith—[27]to the only wise God be glory forevermore through Jesus Christ! Amen.
>
> Romans 16:25–27

These verses are a doxology. Paul begins, "Now to him who is able to strengthen you . . ." But he gets so caught up in God that he does not come down again to the words of the doxology until verse 27: "to the only wise God be glory forevermore through Jesus Christ! Amen."

Sandwiched inside the two parts of the doxology is a massive statement about the meaning of Paul's gospel in relation to God's eternal purposes. The thought moves as follows. The strength that Paul prays will come to the Romans (25a) accords with his gospel and the preaching of Christ (25b). This means that God's power is revealed in the gospel Paul preaches, and that's the power he prays for them to be strengthened by.

Then he says that this gospel preaching is in accord with the revelation of a mystery kept secret for ages and now revealed (25c, 26a). In other words, what Paul preaches is not out of sync with God's purposes. It "accords" with them. It expresses and conforms to them. His preaching is a part of God's plan that is now being revealed in history.

How is it being revealed? It is being disclosed through the prophetic writings (26b). This means that the mystery was not *totally* hidden in past ages. There were pointers in the prophetic writings. So much so that now these very Old Testament writings are used to make the mystery known. (See, for example, how Paul does this in Romans 15:9–13). In Paul's preaching of the gospel, he uses the prophetic writings to help him make known the mystery.

What then is the mystery? Verse 26c–26d says that making known this mystery accords with "the command of the eternal God to bring about the obedience of faith" in all the nations. The most natural way to interpret this is to say that the mystery is the purpose of God to command all nations to obey him through faith.

But what makes this a mystery is that the command to the nations for the obedience of faith is specifically a command to have faith in Jesus the Messiah of Israel, and thus become part of the people of God and heirs of Abraham (Eph. 2:19–3:6). In Romans 1:5, Paul describes his calling to the nations with these words: "We have received grace and apostleship to bring about the obedience of faith for the sake of [Christ's] name among all the nations." Here he makes plain that the aim "to bring about the obedience of faith" in Romans 16:26d is a call for the sake of Christ's name. It is thus a call to acknowledge and trust and obey Christ. This is the mystery hidden for ages—that all the nations would be commanded to trust in Israel's Messiah and be saved through him.

The word "now" in 26a is crucial ("but has *now* been disclosed"). It refers to the "fullness of time" in redemptive history when God put Christ forward onto the center stage of history (Gal. 4:4). From "now" on things are different. The time has come for the mystery to be revealed. The time has come to command all the nations to obey God through faith in Jesus the Messiah.

God is "now" doing a new thing. With the coming of Christ, God will no longer "allow . . . the nations to walk in their own ways" (Acts 14:16, see below). The time has come for all nations to be called to repent, and for the mystery to be fully revealed that through faith in Christ the nations are "fellow heirs, members of the same body, and partakers of the promise in Christ Jesus *through the gospel*" (Eph. 3:6). Not *without* the gospel! But *through* the gospel. This will become increasingly obvious and crucial as we move on.

"The Times of Ignorance"

In Paul's sermon to the Greeks on the Areopagus in Athens, he refers to "the times of ignorance." What did he mean?

> The times of ignorance God overlooked, but now he commands all people everywhere to repent, because he has fixed a day on which he will judge the world in righteousness by a man whom he has appointed; and of this he has given assurance to all by raising him from the dead.
>
> Acts 17:30–31

Paul had noticed an "altar . . . '[t]o the unknown god.'" So he said, "What therefore you worship as unknown, this I proclaim to you" (Acts 17:23). In other words, just in case there was another god in the universe which they did not know anything about, nor had ever heard of, they put up an altar, hoping that this "unknowing" act of homage would be acceptable to this deity.

It would be going too far to say that Paul means there was true esteeming of the true God going on in the building of this altar. One cannot truly esteem what one knows nothing about. The worshiping of the "unknown god" was simply a polytheistic admission that there may be another deity unknown to them whose favor, if he exists, they would like to have. This "ignorant" worship is one thing that makes the past generations to be "times of ignorance" (v. 30). And we will see that even when there is some knowledge of the true God (as in the case of Cornelius in Acts 10), the worship of the true God "ignorantly" is *not* a saving act.

The "times of ignorance" in Paul's sermon correspond to the ages in which "the mystery of Christ" has been kept secret (Rom. 16:25; Col. 1:26; Eph. 3:5). These are the times in which, according to Acts 14:16, God has "allowed all the nations to walk in their own ways." Or as Acts 17:30 says, the times that God "overlooked."

What Does *Overlooking* Mean?

God's *overlooking* "the times of ignorance" does not mean that he ignores sins so as not to punish them. This would contradict Romans 1:18 ("the wrath of God is revealed from heaven against all ungodliness and unrighteousness of men") and Romans 2:12 ("all who have sinned without the law will also perish without the law").

Rather, God's overlooking "the times of ignorance" refers to his giving men over to their own ways. His "overlooking" is his sovereign decision to postpone an all-out pursuit of their repentance through the mission of his people. Calvin explains it this way: "The reason why men have wandered from the truth for so long is that God did not stretch forth His hand from heaven to lead them back to the way. . . . Ignorance was rampant in the world, as long as it pleased God to take no notice of it."[4]

This does not mean that the commands and instructions were not there in the Old Testament for Israel to bear witness to the nations of the grace of God and invite their participation in ways appropriate to that time in redemptive history (e.g., Ps. 67; Gen. 12:2–3). It means rather that, for generations, God did not intervene to purify and empower and commission his people with the incarnation, crucifixion, Great Commission, and outpouring of Pentecostal power to fulfill it. Instead, for his own wise purposes, he "allowed all the nations to walk in their own ways" (Acts 14:16)—and allowed his own nation to experience extended failures of reverence and holiness and love so that they would come to see the full need of a Redeemer from the corruption of sin, and from the curse of the law, and from the limitations of the old covenant for world evangelization.

4. John Calvin, *The Acts of the Apostles 14–28*, trans. John W. Fraser (Grand Rapids: Eerdmans, 1973), 123.

God's ways are not our ways. Even today we live in a similar time of "hardening"—only now the tables are turned, and it is Israel that is largely passed over for a season.

> Lest you [Gentiles] be wise in your own sight, I want you to understand this mystery, brothers: a partial hardening has come upon Israel, until the fullness of the Gentiles has come in. And in this way all Israel will be saved.
>
> Romans 11:25–26

There was a time when the Gentiles were passed over while God dealt with Israel, and now there is a time while Israel is largely passed over as God gathers the full number of his elect from the nations. This does not mean that we should neglect our mission toward Jew or Gentile that we might "save some of them" (Rom. 11:14; 1 Cor. 9:22). But God has his sovereign purposes in determining who actually hears and believes the gospel. And we may be sure that those purposes are wise and holy and will bring the greatest glory to his name (Isa. 48:11; Rom. 11:36).

What God's Wisdom Does Not Allow

We are given a glimpse of this divine wisdom in 1 Corinthians 1:21: "Since, *in the wisdom of God, the world did not know God through wisdom,* it pleased God through the folly of what we preach to save those who believe." Thus it was God's wisdom that determined that men would not know him through their wisdom. In other words, this is an instance and illustration of how God overlooked (i.e., glanced over) the times of ignorance and allowed men to go their own ways.

Why? To make crystal clear that men on their own, by their own wisdom (religion!), will never truly know God. An extraordinary, special work of God would be required to bring people to a true and saving knowledge of God, namely, the preaching of Christ crucified: "It pleased God through the folly of what we preach to save those who believe."

This is what Paul meant in Ephesians 3:6 when he said that the mystery of Christ is that the nations are becoming partakers of the promise *"through the gospel."* Thus 1 Corinthians 1:21 ("Since, in the wisdom of God, the world did not know God through wisdom, it pleased God through the folly of what we preach to save those who believe") and Ephesians 3:6 ("This mystery is that the Gentiles are fellow heirs, members of the same body, and partakers of the promise in Christ Jesus through the gospel") are parallel ideas, and utterly crucial for seeing that in this "now" of redemptive history, knowing the gospel is the only way to become an heir of the promise.

All boasting is excluded by God's showing that man's own wisdom among all the nations—his own self-wrought religions—does not bring him to God. Rather, God saves now by means of preaching that is "a stumbling block to Jews and folly to Gentiles, but to those who are called, both Jews and Greeks, Christ the power of God and the wisdom of God" (1 Cor.

1:23–24). In this way, all boasting is excluded. For left to himself, man does not come to God.

William Carey's Explanation of God's Delay

In his inspiring book *A Vision for Missions*, Tom Wells tells the story of how William Carey illustrated this conviction in his own preaching. Carey was an English Baptist missionary, who left for India in 1793. He never came home, but persevered for forty years in the gospel ministry.

> Once he was talking with a Brahman in 1797. The Brahman was defending idol worship, and Carey cited Acts 14:16 and 17:30.
> God formerly "suffered all nations to walk in their own ways," said Carey, "but now commandeth all men everywhere to repent."
> "Indeed," said the native, "I think God ought to repent for not sending the gospel sooner to us."
> Carey was not without an answer. He said,
> Suppose a kingdom had been long overrun by the enemies of its true king, and he though possessed of sufficient power to conquer them, should yet suffer them to prevail, and establish themselves as much as they could desire, would not the valour and wisdom of that king be far more conspicuous in exterminating them, than it would have been if he had opposed them at first, and prevented their entering the country? Thus by the diffusion of gospel light, the wisdom, power, and grace of God will be more conspicuous in overcoming such deep-rooted idolatries, and in

destroying all that darkness and vice which have so universally prevailed in this country, than they would have been if all had not been suffered to walk in their own ways for so many ages past.[5]

Carey's answer to why God allowed nations to walk in their own ways is that in doing so the final victory of God will be all the more glorious. There is a divine wisdom in the timing of God's deliverances from darkness. We should humble ourselves to see it, rather than presume to know better how God should deal with a rebellious world.

Assessing the Worth of Ignorant Worship

In Acts 17:30, how does Paul assess the ignorant worship of the unknown god (17:23)? He says that the time has come for repentance in view of the impending judgment of the world by Jesus Christ ("He has fixed a day on which he will judge the world in righteousness by a man whom he has appointed," Acts 17:31). In other words, Paul does not reveal to the worshipers in Athens that they are already prepared to meet their Judge because they render a kind of worship through their altar to the unknown god (17:23). They are not ready. They must repent.

As Jesus said in Luke 24:47, from the time of the resurrection onward "*repentance* and forgiveness of

5. Tom Wells, *A Vision for Missions* (Edinburgh: Banner of Truth Trust, 1985), 12–13.

sins should be preached *in his name* to all nations." What is to be preached is that through confessing the name of Jesus, sins can be forgiven. This was not known before, because Jesus was not here before. But now the times of ignorance are over. Jesus has brought the purposes of God to fulfillment. In him all the promises are yes (2 Cor. 1:20). At his throne every knee will bow. Therefore, henceforth he is the focus of saving faith. He is now openly installed and declared as Judge, and he alone can receive the appeals for acquittal.

Summing Up

What then are we saying so far? We are saying that the coming of Jesus Christ into the world is an event of such stupendous proportions that a change has occurred in the necessary focus of saving faith. Before his coming, saving faith reposed in the forgiving and helping mercy of God displayed in events like the exodus and in the sacrificial offerings and in the prophetic promises like Isaiah 53. Jesus was not known personally or by name. The mystery that the nations would be fully included through the preaching of *his name* was kept secret for ages. Those were times of ignorance. God let the nations go their own way.

But "now"—a key word in the turning of God's historic work of redemption—something new has happened. The Son of God has appeared. He has revealed the Father. He has atoned for sin. He has risen from the dead. His authority as universal Judge is vindicated. And the message of his saving work is to be spread to all peoples. This turn in redemptive history is for the glory of Jesus Christ. Its aim is to put him at the center of all God's saving work. And therefore, it accords with this purpose that henceforth Christ be the sole and necessary focus of saving faith. Apart from a knowledge of him, none who has the ability to know will be saved.[6]

Taking the Turn in History Seriously

This tremendously important turn in redemptive history from "the times of ignorance" and the hiddenness of "the mystery of Christ" is not taken seriously enough by those who say people can be saved *today* who do not know Christ because people were saved

---

6. I state it like this so as to leave open salvation for infants and the disabled who do not have the physical ability to even apprehend that there is any revelation available at all. The principle of accountability in Romans 1:20 (God makes knowledge available "so they are without excuse") is the basis for this conviction. The Bible does not deal with this special case in any detail, and we are left to speculate that the fitness of the connection between faith in Christ and salvation will be preserved through the coming to faith of children whenever God brings them to maturity in heaven or in the age to come. But let it be clear that the case of an infant and a profoundly mentally disabled adult is *not* analogous to a healthy adult who has never heard the gospel of Christ. The point of Romans 1:18–21 is that ordinary adults everywhere all have access, because of their eyes and ears and minds, to God's natural revelation but suppress it. Infants and the profoundly disabled do not have the mental and sensory framework for receiving natural revelation. For a defense of this view, see Ronald H. Nash, *When a Baby Dies: Answers to Comfort Grieving Parents* (Grand Rapids: Zondervan, 1999).

in the Old Testament who did not know Christ. For example, Millard Erickson argues this way but does not reckon seriously enough with the tremendous significance that the New Testament sees in the historical turning point of the incarnation that ends "the times of ignorance" and manifests "the mystery of Christ."

> If Jews possessed salvation in the Old Testament era simply by virtue of having the form of the Christian gospel without its content, can this principle be extended? Could it be that those who ever since the time of Christ have had no opportunity to hear the gospel, as it has come through the special revelation, participate in this salvation on the same basis?[7]

This would be a valid argument perhaps if the New Testament did not teach that the coming of Christ is a decisive turn in redemptive history that henceforth makes him the focus of all saving faith.

But is this conclusion supported by other New Testament teaching? What about the case of Cornelius? Was he not a Gentile, living after the resurrection of Christ and saved through his genuine piety without focusing his faith on Christ?

7. Erickson, "Hope for Those Who Haven't Heard? Yes, But . . . ," 124–25.

5

Is Conscious Faith in Jesus Necessary for Salvation?

Part Two: The Case of Cornelius

The story of Cornelius, the Gentile centurion, in Acts 10 could lead some to believe that a man can be saved today apart from knowing the gospel and just by fearing God and doing the good that he can.[1]

1. Ralph Winter wrote letters to Arthur Glasser on September 27, 2003, and to David Hesselgrave on July 4, 2004, disagreeing with both of them and arguing that Cornelius could find repentance unto life and be saved without hearing about Jesus and believing the gospel, because he had access to the Old Testament. Hesselgrave, in an unmentioned publication, and Glasser, in his book *Announcing the Kingdom: The Story of God's Mission in the Bible* (Grand Rapids: Baker, 2003), 276–78, had both argued that Cornelius needed to hear and believe the gospel in order to be saved. They based this in part on Acts 11:13–14: "Send to Joppa and bring Simon who is called Peter; he will declare

Cornelius is described as "a devout man who feared God with all his household, gave alms generously to the people, and prayed continually to God" (10:2). On one occasion an angel says to him, "Cornelius, your prayer has been heard and your alms have been remembered before God. Send therefore to Joppa and ask for Simon who is called Peter" (10:31–32).

Meanwhile, the apostle Peter has had a vision from the Lord designed to teach him that the ceremonial uncleanness of the Gentiles is not a hindrance to their acceptance by God. A voice said to Peter, "What God has made clean, do not call common" (10:15).

When Peter meets Cornelius, he says, "Truly I understand that God shows no partiality, but in every nation anyone who fears him and does what is right is acceptable to him" (10:34–35). This is the sentence that might lead some to think that Cornelius was already saved from his sin even before he heard and believed the gospel. But in fact, Luke's point in telling the story seems to be just the opposite.

It will be helpful to ask two questions that are really pressing in this story. One is this: Was Cornelius already saved before Peter preached Christ to him? The reason this is so pressing is that verses 34–35 have led many to say that he was. They are the beginning of Peter's sermon: "Truly I understand that God shows

---

to you a message *by which you will be saved*, you and all your household." For the letters Winter sent, see Ralph Winter, *Frontiers in Mission: Discovering and Surmounting Barriers to the* Missio Dei (Pasadena, CA: William Carey International University Press, 2008), 161–63.

no partiality, but in every nation anyone who fears him and does what is right is acceptable to him."

You can see how readers would easily conclude that Cornelius was already saved since verse 2 said that he indeed feared God and prayed and gave alms. Did Peter then just inform Cornelius about the acceptance and salvation that he already had? And can we draw the conclusion for missions that there are unreached people who already have a saving relationship with God before they hear the gospel of Jesus?

My second question will assume the answer to this first one and bring us to the very pointed application of this story to world missions. But my first question is: Does verse 35 mean that Cornelius and people like him are already in God's family and justified and reconciled to God and saved from wrath? Is that Peter's point in saying this and Luke's point in writing it?

Was Cornelius Already Saved?

Let me give you four reasons from the text for answering no.

1. Acts 11:14 says that the message Peter brought was the way Cornelius was saved. Look at 11:13–14 where Peter tells the story of the angel's appearing to Cornelius: "He told us how he had seen the angel stand in his house and say, 'Send to Joppa and bring Simon who is called Peter; he will declare to you *a message by which you will be saved*, you and all your household.'"

Notice two things. First, notice that the message itself is essential. The gospel is the power of God unto salvation. Then notice that the tense of the verb is future: "a message by which you *will* be saved." In other words, the message was not simply the informing of Cornelius that he already was saved. If he sends for Peter and hears the message and believes on the Christ of that message, then he *will* be saved. And if he does not, he won't be.

This surely is why the whole story is built around God's miraculously getting Cornelius and Peter together. There was a message that Cornelius needed to hear to be saved (10:22, 33). So Acts 10:35 ("anyone who fears [God] and does what is right is acceptable to him") probably does not mean that Cornelius is already saved when it says that people in unreached ethnic groups who fear God and do right are acceptable to God. Cornelius had to hear the gospel message to be saved.

2. Peter makes this point at the end of his sermon in 10:43. He brings the message to a close with these words: "To him [Christ] all the prophets bear witness that *everyone who believes in him receives forgiveness of sins through his name.*"

Forgiveness of sins is salvation. No one is saved whose sins against God are not forgiven by God. And Peter says that forgiveness comes through believing in Christ, and it comes through the name of Christ.

He does not say, "I am here to announce to you that those of you who fear God and do right are already forgiven." He says, "I am here so that you may hear the gospel and receive forgiveness in the name of Christ by believing in him." So again it is very unlikely that verse 35 means that Cornelius and his household were already forgiven for their sins before they heard the message of Christ.

3. Elsewhere in the book of Acts, even those who are the most God-fearing and ethical, namely, the Jews, are told that they must repent and believe in order to be saved. The Jews at Pentecost were called "devout men" (2:5), like Cornelius was called "a devout man" (10:2). But Peter ended his message in Acts 2 by calling even devout Jews to repent and be baptized in the name of Jesus for the forgiveness of their sins (2:38). The same is true in Acts 3:19 and 13:38–39.

So Luke is not trying to tell us in this book that devout, God-fearing people who practice what's right as best they know how are already saved and without any need of the gospel. The gospel got its start among the most devout people in the world at that time—the Jews. They had more advantages in knowing God than any of the other peoples of the earth. Yet they were told again and again: *Devoutness and works of righteousness and religious sincerity do not solve the problem of sin. The only hope is to believe on Jesus.*

4. The fourth reason for saying that verse 35 does not mean Cornelius and others like him are already saved is found in Acts 11:18. When the people hear Peter tell the story about Cornelius, their initial misgivings are silenced. Luke says, "And they glorified God, saying, 'Then to the Gentiles also God has granted *repentance that leads to life.*'"

This does not mean that the believers concluded that Cornelius had repented before Peter came. The phrase "grant repentance" was used in Acts 5:31 for what happened through the preaching of the apostles first to the Jews and now to the Gentiles: "God exalted [Jesus] at his right hand as Leader and Savior, to *give repentance to Israel* and forgiveness of sins." This, they conclude, is now what has happened to Cornelius and his house. "They glorified God, saying, 'Then to the Gentiles *also* [in addition to Israel in Acts 5:31] God has *granted repentance* that leads to life.'"

In other words, Cornelius and his house did not *already* have eternal life. Repentance *leads to* eternal life (literally, it is "unto eternal life"). They received eternal life when they heard the message about Christ and turned (repented) and believed on him.

So I conclude that when Peter says, "In every nation anyone who fears [God] and does what is right is acceptable to him" in Acts 10:35, he does not mean that Cornelius was already saved. That's the answer to my first question.

How Was Cornelius "Acceptable" to God?

The second question is simply: What then does it mean when Peter says, "In every nation anyone who fears [God] and does what is right is acceptable to him" (10:35)? And what does this have to do with our commitment to world evangelization?

In trying to answer this question, my first thought was that what Peter means in verse 35 is what God meant in the vision about the unclean animals, namely, the lesson of verse 15: "What God has made clean, do not call common"? But something stopped me and made me think again.

"Acceptable" Does Not Mean What All People Are

Consider verse 28. Peter is explaining to the Gentiles why he was willing to come and says, "You yourselves know how unlawful it is for a Jew to associate with or to visit anyone of another nation, but God has shown me that I should not call *any person* common or unclean."

What this means is that Christians should never look down on a person from any race or ethnic group and say that they are unfit to hear the gospel. Or that such people are too unclean for us to go into their house to share the gospel. Or that they are not worth evangelizing. Or that they have too many offensive habits to even get near them.

But the phrase that makes verse 28 so powerful is the phrase "any person" or "anyone": "God has shown me that I should not call any person common or unclean." In other words, Peter learned from his vision on the housetop in Joppa that God rules no one out of his favor on the basis of race or ethnic origin or mere cultural or physical distinctives. "Common or unclean" meant *rejected, despised, taboo*. It was like leprosy.

And Peter's point here in verse 28 is that there is not one human being on the face of the earth that we should think about that way. Not one. That's the amazing thing in Acts 10:28. Our hearts should go out to every single person whatever the color, whatever the ethnic origin, whatever the physical traits, whatever the cultural distinctives. We are not to write off anybody. "God has shown me that I should not call anyone—not one—common or unclean."

"Acceptable" Is Something More

Now that is *not* what Peter says in verse 35. This is what kept me from assuming that verse 35 simply meant that all people are acceptable as candidates for salvation, no matter their ethnic background. In verse 35, Peter says, "*In* every nation [note the word "in"] anyone who fears him and does what is right is acceptable to him." Here he is not talking about every person, like he was in verse 28. Here he is talking about *some* in every nation. "*In* every nation anyone who fears him and does what is right is acceptable to him."

So the acceptability Peter has in mind here is something more, it seems, than merely not being common or unclean—that's everybody. Peter said, Do not "call *any person* common or unclean." Here he says that only *some* in every nation fear God and do right. And these are acceptable to God.

So now we know two things which verse 35 does not mean. (1) It does not mean that these God-fearing doers of good are saved. We saw four reasons why it can't mean that. And (2) it does not mean merely that they are acceptable candidates for evangelism (not common or unclean, not taboo), because verse 28 already said that's true of *everybody*, not just *some*. But verse 35 says that only some "in every nation" are God-fearing, doing what is right and thus acceptable to God.

So the meaning probably lies somewhere between these two—between being saved and being a touchable, lovable human candidate for evangelism.

My suggestion is that Cornelius represents a kind of unsaved person among an unreached people group who is seeking God in an extraordinary way. And Peter is saying that God *accepts* this search as genuine (hence "acceptable" in verse 35) and works wonders to bring that person the gospel of Jesus Christ the way he did through the visions of both Peter on the housetop and Cornelius in the hour of prayer.

A Modern Cornelius

This "extraordinary searching" still happens today. Don Richardson, in his book *Eternity in Their Hearts*, tells of a conversion very similar to Cornelius's. The Gedeo people of south-central Ethiopia were a tribe of a half-million coffee-growing people who believed in a benevolent being called *Magano*, the omnipotent Creator of all that is. Few of the Gedeo people prayed to Magano, being concerned instead to appease an evil being they called *Sheit'an*. But one Gedeo man,

Warrasa Wanga, from the town of Dilla on the edge of Gedeo tribal land, prayed to Magano to reveal himself to the Gedeo people.

Then Warrasa Wanga had a vision: Two white-skinned strangers came and built flimsy shelters for themselves under the shade of a sycamore tree near Dilla. Later they built more permanent shiny-roofed structures which eventually dotted an entire hillside. Warrasa had never seen anything like these structures, since all of the Gedeo dwellings were grass-roofed. Then Warrasa heard a voice say, "These men will bring you a message from Magano, the God you seek. Wait for them." In the last scene of his vision, Warrasa saw himself remove the center pole from his own house, carry it out of the town, and set it in the ground next to one of the shiny-roofed dwellings of the men. In Gedeo symbolism, the center pole of a man's house stands for his very life.

Eight years later, in December, 1948, two Canadian missionaries, Albert Brant and Glen Cain, came to Ethiopia to begin a work among the Gedeo people. They intended to ask permission from Ethiopian officials to place their new mission in the center of the Gedeo region, but they were advised by other Ethiopians that their request would be refused due to the current political climate. The advisors told them to ask permission only to go as far as Dilla, on the extreme edge of Gedeo tribal land. Permission was granted, and when they reached Dilla, the missionaries set up their tents under an old sycamore tree.

Thirty years later, there were more than 200 churches among the Gedeo people, with each church averaging more than 200 members.[2] Almost the entire Gedeo tribe has been influenced by the gospel. Warrasa was one of the first converts, and the first to be imprisoned for his faith.[3]

The Fear of God That Is Acceptable to God

The main evidence that Luke is talking about this kind of "acceptable" unsaved person who seeks the true God and his messengers is found in verses 31–32 where Cornelius says that the angel said to him, "Cornelius, *your prayer has been heard* and your alms have been remembered before God. Send *therefore* to Joppa and ask for Simon who is called Peter." Notice: Your prayers have been heard . . . *therefore* send for Peter. This implies that the prayers were for God to send him what he needed in order to be saved.

So the fear of God that is acceptable to God in verse 35 is a true sense that there is a holy God, that we have to meet him some day as desperate sinners, that we cannot save ourselves and need to know God's way of salvation, and that we pray for it day and night and seek to act on the light we have. This is what Cornelius was doing. And God accepted his prayer and his

2. Don Richardson, *Eternity in Their Hearts* (Ventura, CA.: Regal Books, 1981), 56–58.

3. W. Harold Fuller, *Run While the Sun Is Hot* (Chicago: Moody, 1968), 183–84.

groping for truth in his life (Acts 17:27) and worked wonders to bring the saving message of the gospel to him. Cornelius would not have been saved if no one had taken him the gospel. And no one who can apprehend revelation (see note 2, chapter 5) will be saved today without the gospel.

Therefore, Cornelius does not represent persons who are saved without hearing and believing the gospel; rather, he illustrates God's intention to take out a people for his name from "every nation" (Acts 10:35) through the sending of gospel messengers across cultural boundaries which had once been taboo.

We should learn with the Jewish church in Jerusalem that "to the Gentiles also God has granted repentance that leads to life" (11:18). But we must be sure that we learn this the way they learned it: they inferred this from the fact that the Gentiles *believed the gospel that Peter preached* and received the Holy Spirit. They did not infer the acceptance of the Gentiles from their fear of God and their good deeds, even when that was rooted in the Old Testament, as it probably was for a God-fearer like Cornelius.

It appears, therefore, that Luke's intention in telling the Cornelius story is to show that Gentiles can become part of the chosen people of God through faith in Jesus in spite of their ceremonial "uncleanness." The point is *not* that Gentiles are already part of God's chosen people because they fear God. The key sentence is Acts 11:14—"He will declare to you a *message by which you will be saved.*"

6

Is Conscious Faith in Jesus Necessary for Salvation?

Part Three: No Other Name under Heaven

The previous chapter closed with the assertion that people are saved through the message of the gospel. "He will declare to you a *message* by which you will be saved" (Acts 11:14). The reason this message is actually a *saving* message is that the message proclaims the *name* that saves—the name of Jesus. Peter said that God visited the Gentiles "to take from them a people *for his name*" (Acts 15:14). It stands to reason then that the proclamation by which God takes a people for his name would be a message that hinges on the name of his Son, Jesus.

This is, in fact, what we saw in Peter's preaching at the house of Cornelius. The sermon comes to its climax with these words about Jesus: "Everyone who believes in him receives forgiveness of sins *through his name*" (Acts 10:43).

Peter's Other Sermon—No Other Name

The implicit necessity of hearing and embracing the name of Jesus, which we see in the story of Cornelius, is made explicit in Acts 4:12 in the climax of another sermon by Peter, this time before the Jewish rulers in Jerusalem:

> And there is salvation in no one else, for there is no other name under heaven given among men by which we must be saved.

The situation behind this famous sentence is that the risen Jesus healed a man through the apostles Peter and John. The man had been lame from birth, but he got up and ran through the temple praising God. A crowd gathered, and Peter preached (Acts 3). His message makes it obvious that what is at stake here is not merely a local religious phenomenon. It has to do with everybody in the world.

Then, according to Acts 4:1, the priests and the captain of the temple and the Sadducees came and arrested Peter and John and put them in custody overnight. The next morning the rulers and elders and scribes gathered and interrogated Peter and John. In the course of the interrogation, Peter drew out the implication of the universal lordship of Jesus: "There is salvation in no one else, for there is no other name under heaven given among men by which we must be saved."

The Universality of the Claim

We need to feel the force of this universal claim by taking several phrases very seriously. The reason there is salvation in no one else is that "there is no other name *under heaven* [not just no other name in Israel, but no other name *under heaven*, including the heaven over Greece and Rome and Spain] given *among men* [not just among Jews, but among all humans everywhere] by which we must be saved." These two phrases, "under heaven" and "among men," press the claim of universality to its fullest extent.

But there is even more here that we need to see. Commentators usually interpret Acts 4:12 to mean that without believing in Jesus a person cannot be saved. In other words, Acts 4:12 is seen as a crucial text in answering the question whether those who have never heard the gospel of Jesus can be saved.

Does Acts 4:12 Have Relevance for Those Who Have Never Heard?

But Clark Pinnock represents others who say that "Acts 4:12 does not say anything about [this question].

. . . It does not comment on the fate of the heathen. Although it is a question of great importance to us, it is not one on which Acts 4:12 renders a judgment, either positive or negative."[1] Rather, what Acts 4:12 says is that "salvation in its fullness is available to humankind only because God in the person of his Son Jesus provided it."[2]

In other words, the verse says that salvation comes only through the *work* of Jesus but not only through faith in Jesus. His work can benefit those who relate to God properly without him, for example, on the basis of general revelation in nature.

The problem with Pinnock's interpretation is that it does not reckon with the true significance of Peter's focus on the "name" of Jesus. "There is no other *name* under heaven *by which* we must be saved." Peter is saying something more than that there is no other *source* of saving power by which you can be saved under some *other* name. The point of saying, "There is no other *name*," is that we are saved by calling on the name of the Lord Jesus. Calling on his name is our entrance into fellowship with God. If one is saved by Jesus incognito, one does not speak of being saved *by his name*.

We noticed above that Peter said in Acts 10:43, "Everyone *who believes in him* receives forgiveness of sins *through his name*." The name of Jesus is the focus

1. Pinnock, "Acts 4:12—No Other Name under Heaven," 110. Pinnock acknowledges that the commentators (e.g., Bruce, Haenchen, Longenecker, Conzelmann) take Acts 4:12 to support the "exclusivist paradigm."

2. Ibid., 109.

of faith and repentance. In order to believe on Jesus for the forgiveness of sins, you must believe on his name. Which means that you must have heard of him and know who he is as a particular man who did a particular saving work and rose from the dead.

The point of Acts 4:12 for missions is made explicit by the way Paul picks up on this very issue of "the name of the Lord" Jesus in Romans 10:13–15. We turn to this passage now and see that missions is essential precisely because "'everyone who calls on *the name of the Lord* will be saved.' How then will they call on him in whom they have not believed? And how are they to believe in him of whom they have never heard? And how are they to hear without someone preaching?"

"How Are They to Believe in Him of Whom They Have Never Heard?"

In Romans 10:13, Paul makes the great gospel declaration, quoting Joel 2:32, "Everyone who calls on the name of the Lord will be saved." He follows this with rhetorical questions, "How then will they call on him in whom they have not believed? And how are they to believe in him of whom they have never heard?" These are extremely important words relating to the necessity of the missionary enterprise.

Consider the context of these words in Romans 9:30–10:21. Paul begins and ends this unit by saying: Gentiles, who never had the advantages of God's revealed law, have nevertheless attained a right standing with God—through Christ—while Israel, with all her advantages, has not attained a right standing with God.

Here is how he says it in Romans 9:30–31: "Gentiles who did not pursue righteousness have attained it, that is, a righteousness that is by faith; but . . . Israel who pursued a law that would lead to righteousness did not succeed in reaching that law." And here is how he says it in Romans 10:20–21: "Then Isaiah is so bold as to say, 'I have been found by those who did not seek me; I have shown myself to those who did not ask for me.' But of Israel he says, 'All day long I have held out my hands to a disobedient and contrary people.'"

Paul is burdened to show that the great reason for this strange reversal—Gentiles getting right with God and actually fulfilling the demands of the law of God, but Israel failing with their own law to get right with God—is that "the goal of the law is Christ for righteousness for everyone who believes" (Rom. 10:4, my literal translation). Israel missed the point of their own law—namely, to point them to Christ and the way of justification by faith as the only hope of fulfilling the law (9:32). And then, when Christ appeared, they "stumbled over the stumbling stone" (9:32). They would not "submit to God's righteousness" (10:3). But Gentiles embraced the promise, "Whoever believes in him will not be put to shame" (9:33).

Paul makes the transition to the New Testament gospel, and the missionary setting of his life, in chapter 10, verse 8 when he says that the message of the Old Testament law, pointing to Christ the Redeemer, is "the word of faith that we proclaim." Then he says explicitly that this Redeemer is Jesus and that all salvation now is by confessing him—just as salvation in the Old Testament was by embracing the pointers to his coming and banking on God's saving grace that he would one day purchase. Thus verse 9 says, "If you confess with your mouth that *Jesus is Lord* and believe in your heart that God raised him from the dead, you will be saved."

Paul underlines that salvation through believing and confessing Jesus as Lord was the Old Testament hope. He does this by quoting Isaiah 28:16 in Romans 10:11 ("For the Scripture says, 'Everyone who believes in him will not be put to shame'") and by quoting Joel 2:32 in Romans 10:13 ("Everyone who calls on the name of the Lord will be saved").

So when Romans 10:11 quotes Isaiah 28:16, "Everyone who believes in him will not be put to shame," the reference is clearly to Jesus, the predicted cornerstone. And when 10:13 quotes Joel 2:32, "Everyone who calls upon the name of the Lord will be saved," Jesus is the "Lord" referred to, even though in Joel 2:32 "Yahweh" is in view. The reason we know this is that 10:9 said, "If you confess with your mouth that *Jesus* is Lord . . . you will be saved."

So Paul is making clear that in this new era of redemptive history, Jesus is the goal and climax of Old Testament teaching, and therefore Jesus now stands as Mediator between man and Yahweh as the object of saving faith.

A Difficult Flow But Clear Outcome

The flow of thought from Romans 10:14–21 is not easy to grasp. The sequence of questions in verses 14–15 is very familiar and is often cited in relation to missionary work:

> How then [or therefore] will they call on him in whom they have not believed? And how are they to believe in him of whom they have never heard?[3] And how are they to hear without someone preaching? And how are they to preach unless they are sent? As it is written, "How beautiful are the feet of those who preach the good news!"

But how do these verses fit into the flow of Paul's thought? Why do the questions in these verses begin with the word "then" (or "therefore," *oun*)? How does asking a series of questions communicate an *inference*? Why does the next verse (v. 16) begin with "*But* [or *nevertheless*] they have not all obeyed the gospel"?

The answer seems to be this: The "therefore" at the beginning of verse 14 and the "nevertheless" at the beginning of verse 16 point to the fact that the series of questions in verses 14–15 is really making a statement to the effect that God has already worked to bring about these conditions for calling on the Lord Jesus for salvation. We could paraphrase as follows:

3. The Greek verb for "hear" (*akouō*) followed by a person in the genitive case means hear the person, not merely hear *about* him. Most commentators are agreed on this (e.g., Meyer, Murray, Cranfield, Moo).

(10–13) Salvation is richly available to both Jews and Gentiles—to everyone who calls upon the name of the Lord Jesus. (14–15) *Therefore*, God has taken steps to provide the prerequisites for calling on the Lord. He is sending those who preach so that Christ can be heard and people can believe and call on the Lord Jesus. (16) Nevertheless, this has not led to obedience, as Isaiah predicted: "Lord, who has believed our report?"

So far then, the main point of verses 14–16 would be that *even though* God has taken steps to provide the prerequisites for calling on the Lord, *nevertheless* most have not obeyed.

But who is in view here when Paul says they have not believed? The answer to this question divides two different ways of construing Paul's line of reasoning in the whole passage. John Murray and Charles Hodge represent these two lines.

Murray and Hodge Differ, but Not on the Key Issue

Murray says, "At verse 16 the apostle returns to that subject which permeates this section of the epistle, the unbelief of Israel."[4] Similarly, Murray says the focus on Israel's unbelief continues to the end of the paragraph. So, for example, verse 18 also refers to Israel, "But I ask, have they not heard? Indeed they have, for

4. John Murray, *The Epistle to the Romans* (Grand Rapids: Eerdmans, 1965), 2:60.

'Their voice has gone out to all the earth, and their words to the ends of the world.'" He says the quote from Psalm 19:4 (which originally referred to works of nature declaring God's glory) is used by Paul to describe the worldwide spread of the gospel of Jesus. And the point is that if the gospel is going out to all the world, "it cannot then be objected that Israel did not hear."[5] So the focus stays on Israel. The point of Paul's thought throughout Romans 10 is that Israel knows the gospel and is nevertheless rejecting it and is thus accountable.

Charles Hodge, on the other hand, sees the focus differently in verses 11–21. "Paul's object in the whole context is to vindicate the propriety of extending the gospel call to all nations." He sees both verses 16 and 18 as references not to Israel but to the nations. "The 16th verse refers to the Gentiles, 'They have not all obeyed the gospel,' and therefore this verse [18], 'Have they not heard?' cannot, without any intimation of change, be naturally referred to a different subject. . . . In the following verse [19], where the Jews are really intended, they are distinctly mentioned, 'Did not Israel know?'"[6]

In spite of this difference between Murray and Hodge, the important thing for our purpose remains fairly clear, and both agree. Whether Paul is focusing in a narrower way on the accountability of Israel or more broadly on the availability of the gospel to the

5. Ibid., 2:62.

6. Charles Hodge, *Commentary on the Epistle to the Romans* (New York: A. C. Armstrong and Son, 1893), 548.

nations (and therefore also to Israel), both agree that calling on the name of the Lord Jesus is necessary for salvation ("Everyone who calls on the name of the Lord will be saved," 10:13).

Calling on the Lord Jesus Is Essential—Hence the Beautiful Feet of Missionaries

So necessary is it to call on the name of Jesus that Paul feels compelled to show that all the necessary prerequisites for calling on the Lord are being put in place by God (vv. 14–15). Even more relevant for our immediate question is the implication that "calling on the Lord" in a saving way is not something that a person can do from a position of ignorance. One cannot do it from another religion. This is made plain in the questions of verses 14–15.

Each succeeding question rules out an argument from those who say that there can be salvation without hearing the gospel of Jesus. First, "How then will they call on him in whom they have not believed?" shows that effective calling presupposes faith in the one called. This rules out the argument that one might call on God savingly without faith in Christ.

Second, "And how are they to believe in him of whom they have never heard?" shows that faith presupposes hearing Christ in the message of the gospel. This rules out the argument that a person might have saving faith without really knowing or meeting Christ in the gospel.

Third, "And how are they to hear without someone preaching?" shows that hearing Christ in the gospel presupposes a proclaimer of the gospel. This rules out the argument that one might somehow meet Christ or hear Christ without a messenger to tell the gospel.

"Their Voice Has Gone Out to All the Earth"

Millard Erickson does not seem to take the force of this sequence seriously enough when he suggests that the quote from Psalm 19:4 in Romans 10:18 teaches that general revelation in nature is all that some need to receive salvation, apart from missionary proclamation.[7] At first, this suggestion may seem compelling. Paul says that people must hear in order to call on the Lord. Then he asks in verse 18, "Have they not heard?" And he answers with the words of Psalm 19:4: "Indeed they have, for 'Their voice has gone out to all the earth, and their words to the ends of the world.'"

In the original context of Psalm 19, "their voice" and "their words" refer to what is communicated through "night" and "day" and "heavens" and "firmament." So one might conclude that the "hearing" that is necessary for saving faith (Rom. 10:17) is effectively provided through natural revelation. This is what Erickson concludes.[8]

7. See note 19 of chapter 1.

8. Erickson finds support for this conclusion also in Romans 1:18–21. But the problem with this is that although these verses teach the reality of general revelation that is sufficient to hold humanity accountable to glorify God (v. 21), nevertheless they also teach that men suppress this truth in

The problem with this is that it creates an insur-mountable tension with the point of verse 14. There Paul says, "How shall they hear without a preacher?" If Erickson were right that a hearing which is effective to save comes through nature, then Paul's question is misleading: "How are they to hear without someone preaching?" He clearly means that one cannot hear what one needs to hear for salvation unless a preacher is sent. He would contradict this if he meant in verse 18 that preachers are not essential for salvation, be-cause an effective message of salvation comes through nature.

Therefore, as most commentators agree, it is un-likely that Paul intends for verse 18 to teach that natu-ral revelation fulfills the saving role of "the word of Christ" which gives rise to faith (v. 17). Murray and Hodge agree that Paul uses the words of the psalm to draw a parallel between the universality of general revelation and the universal spread of the gospel.[9] The

unrighteousness (v. 18) and do *not* thank God or honor him the way they should (v. 21) and are therefore without excuse (v. 20). General revelation is sufficient to hold all men accountable to worship God but not efficient to bring about the faith that saves. That is why the gospel must be preached to all people. God wills to honor his Son by accompanying the preaching of his name with heart-awakening power.

9. John Murray, *The Epistle to the Romans*, 2:61: "Since the gospel procla-mation is not to all without distinction, it is proper to see the parallel between the universality of general revelation and the universalism of the gospel. The former is the pattern now followed in the sounding forth of the gospel to the uttermost parts of the earth. The application which Paul makes of Psalm 19:4 can thus be seen to be eloquent not only of this parallel but also of that which is implicit in the parallel, namely, the widespread diffusion of the gospel of grace." Charles Hodge, *Commentary on the Epistle to the Romans*,

point is that God has set in motion a missionary movement (the "sending" of verse 15) that will reach to all the peoples of the earth on the analogy of the universal spread of God's glory through natural revelation.[10]

In Sum

Summing up, Peter and Paul are of one mind when you consider the implications of Acts 4:12 and Romans 10:13–21. The issue in both is whether a person can be saved any other way than by calling on the *name*

549: "This verse, therefore is to be considered as a strong declaration that what Paul had proved ought to be done, had in fact been accomplished. The middle wall of partition had been broken down, the gospel of salvation, the religion of God, was free from its trammels, the offers of mercy were as wide and general as the proclamation of the heavens. . . . His object in using the words of the Psalmist was, no doubt, to convey more clearly and affectingly to the minds of his hearers the idea that the proclamation of the gospel was now as free from all nations or ecclesiastical restrictions, as the instructions shed down upon all people by the heavens under which they dwell. Paul, of course, is not to be understood as quoting the Psalmist as though the ancient prophet was speaking of the preaching of the gospel. He simply uses scriptural language to express his own ideas, as is done involuntarily almost by every preacher in every sermon."

10. The words "Their voice has gone out" (Rom. 10:18) do not have to mean that the spread of the message is finished. In Paul's context, the natural meaning is that the gospel has been propelled into the world to reach all peoples. Hermann Olshausen suggests that "their voice has gone out" is to be understood as prophetically spoken: "[T]hat which is begun is viewed as if already completed, and therefore we need not seek for any further explanation how it is that St. Paul can represent Christ's messengers as spread all over the earth, whereas, when he wrote these words, they had not so much as carried the preaching of Christ through the whole of the Roman empire" (Hermann Olshausen, *Studies in the Epistle to the Romans* [Minneapolis: Klock and Klock Christian Publishers, 1983 (1849)], 354).

of the Lord Jesus. Acts 4:12 says, "There is no other *name* under heaven given among men by which we must be saved." And Romans 10:13 says, "Everyone who calls on the *name* of the Lord will be saved," and then describes how God is putting in place the hearing and preaching and sending that make calling on the name of Jesus possible. Both Peter and Paul teach us that hearing about Jesus in the gospel and believing on him and calling on his name are essential for salvation.

The theological assumption behind this apostolic missionary conviction is that Jesus is the fulfillment of all that the Old Testament was pointing toward. Before Jesus, faith was focused on the mercy and promise of God to forgive sins and to care for his people. As revelation progressed, faith could move more easily from the animal sacrifices onto the promised sin-bearer of Isaiah 53.

But when Christ came, all faith narrowed in its focus to him alone as the One who purchased and guaranteed all the hopes of the people of God. From the time of Christ onward, God wills to honor Christ by making him the sole focus of saving faith. Therefore, people must call upon him and believe in him and hear him and be sent messengers with "the word of Christ."

7

Is Conscious Faith in Jesus Necessary for Salvation?

Part Four: The Missionary Task as Seen by Paul and John

The necessity of telling the good news of Jesus to the peoples of the world who have never heard of him, and do not know about his saving work, will now become increasingly plain from the way Paul and John talk about the missionary task itself. Paul speaks out of his own experience of being sent, and John speaks out of his experience of walking with Jesus and hearing the way he spoke of gathering his sheep from outside the Jewish fold.

Paul's Conception of His Own Missionary Vocation

The indispensability of hearing the gospel for salvation is seen in the biblical texts that show us how Paul conceived of his own missionary vocation. At his conversion, Paul received a commission from the Lord that clarifies the condition of those without Christ. He refers to this in Acts 26:15–18:

> And I said, "Who are you, Lord?" And the Lord said, "I am Jesus whom you are persecuting. But rise and stand upon your feet, for I have appeared to you for this purpose, to appoint you as a servant and witness to the things in which you have seen me and to those in which I will appear to you, delivering you from your people and from the Gentiles—to whom *I am sending you to open their eyes, so that they may turn from darkness to light and from the power of Satan to God, that they may receive forgiveness of sins* and a place among those who are sanctified by faith in me."

Here we see what was at stake in Paul's ministry. Without making any exceptions or distinctions, the Lord says that those who do not yet have the gospel are in darkness and in the power of Satan and without the forgiveness of sins. Christ commissioned Paul with a word of power that actually opens the eyes of the spiritually blind, not so that they can see they are forgiven, but so that they can be forgiven. His message delivers from the power of Satan. The picture of nations without the gospel is that of people who are blind and in the darkness and in bondage to Satan and without forgiveness of sins and unacceptable to God because they are unsanctified.

This accords with what Paul says elsewhere about the condition of man without the power of the gospel: all are under sin with their mouths stopped before God (Rom. 3:9–19); they are in the flesh and unable to submit to God or please God (Rom. 8:7–8); they are natural and not spiritual and therefore unable to receive the things of the Spirit (1 Cor. 2:14–16); they are dead in trespasses, and children of wrath (Eph. 2:3–5); and they are darkened in their understanding and alienated from God and hard in heart (Eph. 4:17–18).

Now with the coming of Christ, there is a message that has power to save (Rom. 1:16; 1 Thess. 2:16; 1 Cor. 15:2) and bear fruit (Col. 1:6) and triumph (2 Thess. 3:1), and it is the mission of Paul and all his heirs to preach that message to the nations. "Since, in the wisdom of God, the world did not know God through wisdom [or false religion], it pleased God through the folly of what we preach to save those who believe" (1 Cor. 1:21).

What Is at Stake When Paul Preaches in the Synagogue?

Preaching to Gentiles may be one thing, but when Paul goes and preaches in the synagogue, what is at stake there? Salvation is at stake when Paul speaks to

Jews in the synagogue as well. Paul does not assume that God-fearing Gentiles or Jews are saved by virtue of their knowing the Old Testament Scriptures. What does he say in the synagogue at Antioch of Pisidia?

> Let it be known to you therefore, brothers, that through this man forgiveness of sins is proclaimed to you, and by him every one who believes is freed [literally, *justified*] from everything from which you could not be freed [*justified*] by the law of Moses.
>
> Acts 13:38–39

Paul does not tell even the best of them that they are already forgiven by virtue of their obedience to the law by their faith in the promises without believing in Christ. He offers them forgiveness through Christ. And he makes "freeing" ("justification") from sin conditional upon believing on Christ. When the synagogue later opposes this message, Paul says in Acts 13:46–48,

> "It was necessary that the word of God be spoken first to you. Since you thrust it aside and judge yourselves unworthy of eternal life, behold, we are turning to the Gentiles. For so the Lord has commanded us, saying,
>> "'I have made you a light for the Gentiles,
>>> that you may bring salvation to the ends of the earth.'"
> And when the Gentiles heard this, they began rejoicing and glorifying the word of the Lord, and as many as were appointed to eternal life believed.

Paul's vocation is to bring salvation to the ends of the earth. The assumption is that salvation is not already at the ends of the earth. Paul is to take it. Paul's message is the means of salvation. There is no salvation without it: as many as were ordained to eternal life believed Paul's message, and were saved. God has ordained that salvation come to the nations through sent messengers whose obedient preaching of the gospel brings salvation to the nations.

Through Paul's preaching, God is now doing the sovereign work that he had "overlooked" for so long during "the times of ignorance." He is bringing Gentiles to faith according to his preordained plan. He is opening their hearts to the gospel (Acts 16:14) and granting them repentance (Acts 11:18) and cleansing their hearts by faith (Acts 15:9).

Before this time of gospel privilege, these things were not possible, for God was allowing the nations to go their own way (Acts 14:16). But now a great movement is under way to gather a people for his name from all the nations (Acts 15:14), and God himself is active in the ministry of his messengers to sanctify a people for himself.

God Himself Is the Great Evangelist

This becomes wonderfully clear in Romans 15 where Paul describes his own vocation in its relation to the work of Christ in and through him.

But on some points I have written to you very boldly by way of reminder, because of the grace given me by God to be a minister of Christ Jesus to the Gentiles in the priestly service of the gospel of God, so that the offering of the Gentiles may be acceptable, sanctified by the Holy Spirit. In Christ Jesus, then, I have reason to be proud of my work for God. For I will not venture to speak of anything except what Christ has accomplished through me to bring the Gentiles to obedience—by word and deed.

Romans 15:15–18

Notice the initiative of God in these verses. First, God gave Paul the grace of apostleship and called him to the ministry of the gospel (vv. 15–16). Second, the Gentiles who believe Paul's message are acceptable to God because they are sanctified by the Holy Spirit (v. 16). Third, it is not Paul himself who has won obedience from the Gentiles; it is what Christ has "accomplished through [him]" (v. 18).

So the Gentile mission is the new work of God. It is the fulfillment of divine prophecy that once God allowed the nations to go their own way, but *now* . . .

God . . . visited the Gentiles, to take from them a people for his name. And with this the words of the prophets agree, just as it is written,
> "After this I will return,
>> and I will rebuild the tent of David that
>>> has fallen;
> I will rebuild its ruins,
>> and I will restore it,

111

> that the remnant of mankind may seek the
> Lord,
> > and all the Gentiles who are called by
> > my name,
> > says the Lord, who makes these things
> > known from of old."

Acts 15:14–18

A new day has come with Jesus, the Christ. The people of God are being rebuilt in such a way that they will no longer fail in their task of reaching the nations. In this new day, God will not suffer his people to neglect their mission indefinitely; he will no longer allow the nations to go their own way. He is establishing a church, "that the remnant of mankind may seek the Lord."

And he will now gather in all those among the nations who are called by his name! It is *his* new work! All those who are predestined *will* be called (Rom. 8:30). All those who are foreordained to eternal life *will* believe (Acts 13:48). All those who are ransomed *will* be gathered from every people under heaven (Rev. 5:9). God himself is the chief agent in this new movement, and he *will* take out a people for his name among the nations (Acts 15:14).

What John Tells Us about the Ingathering of Jesus's Sheep

John's conception of the new missionary task parallels Paul's. Just as Paul says no one can believe in a Christ they have not heard (Rom. 10:14), so Jesus says in John 10:27, "My sheep hear my voice, and I know them, and they follow me" (cf. John 10:4, 14). In other words, Jesus gathers his redeemed flock by calling them with his own voice. The true sheep hear his voice and follow, and he gives them eternal life (10:28).

Whom does Jesus have in mind when he speaks of those who will hear his voice and follow him? He means more than the Jews that actually heard him on earth. He says, "I have *other sheep that are not of this fold*. I must bring them also, and they will listen to my voice. So there shall be one flock, one shepherd" (John 10:16). By "other sheep that are not of this fold" he means Gentiles who are not part of the Jewish fold.

But how will these Gentiles hear his voice? The answer is the same as with Paul: they hear the voice of Jesus, not in nature or in an alien religion, but in the voice of Christ's messengers. We see this in the way Jesus prays for his future disciples in John 17:20–21: "I do not ask for these only, but also for those *who will believe in me through their word*, that they may all be one." We infer from this then that "sheep that are not of this fold" will hear the voice of the Shepherd through the voice of his messengers.

So eternal life comes only to those who hear the voice of the Shepherd and follow him. "My sheep hear my voice, and I know them, and they follow me. I give them eternal life" (John 10:27–28). This hearing is through the messengers of the Shepherd.

"I Am the Way. . . . No One Comes to the Father Except through Me"

This is what Jesus meant in John 14:6 when he said, "I am the way, and the truth, and the life. No one comes to the Father except through me." "Through me" does not mean that people in other religions can get to God because Jesus died for them, though they don't know about it. "Through me" must be defined in the context of John's Gospel as believing in Jesus through the word of his disciples (John 6:35; 7:38; 11:25; 12:46; 17:20).

Eternal life is owing to the death of Jesus for his sheep (John 10:15)—a death that atoned not for a few Jewish sheep only but for sheep from every nation. We see this in John 11:51–53 where John interprets the words of Caiaphas, "Being the high priest that year he prophesied that Jesus would die for the nation, *and not for the nation only, but also to gather into one the children of God who are scattered abroad.*"

The "children of God scattered abroad" (11:52) are the "other sheep that are not of this fold" (John 10:16). And when we look at John's picture of the consummation of the missionary cause in Revelation, we see that these "sheep" and "children" are truly from all the nations.

> And they sang a new song, saying,
>> "Worthy are you to take the scroll
>>> and to open its seals,
>> for you were slain, and by your blood you
>>> ransomed people for God

*from every tribe and language and people
and nation,*
and you have made them a kingdom and
priests to our God,
and they shall reign on the earth."

Revelation 5:9–10

Here we see the true extent of the word "scattered" in John 11:52. He died to gather the "children of God" who are "scattered" among "every tribe and language and people and nation."

The implication is that the messengers of the Shepherd *must* (Mark 13:10) and *will* (Matt. 24:14) reach every people under heaven with the message of the gospel and the voice of the Shepherd. The redeemed in heaven from all the peoples are not redeemed without having known and trusted Jesus. Rather, as Revelation 7:14 makes clear, those "from every nation, from all tribes and peoples and languages" (Rev. 7:9) are those who "have washed their robes and made them white in the blood of the Lamb" (Rev. 7:14; cf. 22:14). They are those who "keep the commandments of God and hold to the testimony of Jesus" (Rev. 12:17). The gospel of the blood of Christ crucified for sinners, and risen in victory, must be preached to all the nations so they can believe and be saved.

Paul and John are of one mind: people only come to saving faith through the word of the gospel of Christ. The sheep hear the voice of their Shepherd through the word of those who are sent (John 10:4, 14; 17:20); and Paul knows himself to be sent in this way: "I am sending you to open their eyes, so that they may turn from darkness to light and from the power of Satan to God, that they may receive forgiveness of sins" (Acts 26:17–18). Apart from the work of the Holy Spirit, who works through the word of the gospel of Christ (1 Peter 1:23–25), there is no faith and no new birth and no salvation. This is why "repentance and forgiveness of sins should be proclaimed in his name to all nations" (Luke 24:47).

Conclusion

The question for the church in every generation is: *Will we submit gladly to the Scriptures?* Will we devote ourselves to *understanding* them truly, *valuing* them supremely (under God himself), *applying* them properly, *obeying* them wholeheartedly, and *speaking* them courageously and publicly? In every age, some things in the Bible fit nicely into the spirit of the times and are not controversial. They may even win you some popularity. But in every age, there are other things in the Bible—important things—that do *not* fit the spirit of the times, and speaking them will be criticized or even persecuted.

Will We Love Them?

The world wants to be loved in some of the ways that the Bible commands us to love them. And the world does not want to be loved in other ways that the Bible commands us to love them. Millions of people do not want to be loved by being told that they need to trust Jesus in order to be rescued from everlasting destruction. This seems to them narrow, arrogant, presumptuous, and offensive. This is not new. But it is perhaps more prevalent today than ever.

In the first decades of the twenty-first century, with an ever closer concentration of diverse religions in our urban centers around the world, and with the explosive nearness and immediacy of everything on the internet, more and more Christians are losing the nerve to tell the world—the neighbors at home and the nations who have no gospel access—the good news of Jesus, because they fear it will be heard as intolerant, old-fashioned, arrogant religious dogma.

I have written this little book to convince our minds and strengthen our hearts to do the loving thing, namely, to spread to all peoples the good news of God's work in Jesus to rescue sinners (1 Tim. 1:15; Luke 5:32; Mark 10:45) and someday renew the world (Rom. 8:20–23; 2 Peter 3:13; Rev. 21:1–4). To this end, I have tried to answer three questions with arguments and illustrations from the Bible: Is there an eternal hell of conscious torment to be rescued from? Answer: Yes (Chapter 2). Is the death and resurrection of Christ essential for that rescue? Answer: Yes (Chapter 3). And do people need to hear this good news and believe it in order to be rescued? Answer: Yes (Chapters 4–7).

Are Some Saved without Hearing and Believing Jesus?

The main emphasis has fallen on the last question. To ask it another way: Are some people quickened by the Holy Spirit and saved by grace through faith in a merciful Creator even though they never hear of Jesus in this life? Are there devout people in religions other than Christianity who humbly rely on the grace of a God whom they know only through nature or non-Christian religious experience?

Put this way, the answer of the New Testament is a clear and earnest *no*. The message throughout is that with the coming of Christ a major change has occurred in redemptive history. Saving faith was once focused on the mercy of God known in his redemptive acts among the people of Israel, and in the system of animal sacrifices and in the prophecies of coming redemption.[1]

But *now*, with the coming of the Son of God into the world, the focus of faith has narrowed to one man, Jesus Christ, the fulfillment and guarantee of all redemption and all sacrifices and all prophecies. It is to his honor now that henceforth all saving faith shall be directed to him.

Therefore, this great turn in redemptive history is accompanied by a new mission thrust ordained by God. God no longer allows the nations to walk their own way (Acts 14:16), but sends his messengers everywhere calling all to repent and believe the gospel (Acts 17:30).

---

1. The case of Melchizedek is probably not an exception to this. This mysterious figure who appears in Genesis 14 as a prefiguring of Jesus (Ps. 110:4; Heb. 5:6–10; 6:20; 7:1–17) knows the true God. But we cannot be sure how Melchizedek received his revelation or that he did not depend in some way on the special revelation through the line of Abraham.

God in Christ is himself the power behind this mission. He has ordained his people to life (Acts 13:48) and ransomed them by laying down his life for them (John 10:15; Rev. 5:9). Now he is commissioning Spirit-filled messengers to preach to them (Rom. 10:15; 1:5), and he is speaking through these messengers with power (Luke 12:12; 21:15; 1 Thess. 2:13) and calling the lost effectually to faith (1 Cor. 1:24; Rom. 8:30) and keeping them by his almighty power (Jude 24).

Is the Motivation for Missions Enhanced by Saying Some Don't Have to Hear?

Those who affirm that people who today have no access to the gospel may nevertheless be saved without knowing Jesus try to argue that this idea "enhances our motivation to evangelize the lost." As we saw above, it is a futile effort. The arguments fall apart as you pick them up. For example, John Ellenberger cites four ways our motivation will be "enhanced" by the hope that people may already be saved without faith in Jesus.

1. Citing Acts 18:10 ("I have many in this city who are my people"), he says that "the knowledge that the Holy Spirit has been working in the hearts of people prior to hearing the good news should encourage us."[2] I agree. But that's

---

2. John Ellenberger, "Is Hell a Proper Motivation for Missions?" in Crockett and Sigountos, *Through No Fault of Their Own*, 225.

not the issue. Working in someone's heart to prepare them to respond to the gospel is very different from working in their hearts so that they are saved apart from the gospel. The first motivates missions, the second doesn't.

2. Unintelligibly, he argues that "because the great majority have not responded to general revelation, they need to be confronted by the claims of Jesus."[3] This amounts to saying that if you believe some are saved apart from the claims of special revelation, you will be more motivated to share those claims because most aren't saved that way. A natural interpretation of these words would mean: Where Ellenberger's claim does not apply, there it will increase motivation. This argument is incomprehensible to me.

3. Third, he argues that believing that some are saved apart from the preaching of the gospel "broadens our understanding of the whole gospel."[4] In other words, if we are going to still pursue missions with zeal, it will need to be for reasons wider than merely providing escape from hell (which some already have before we get there). We will need to desire to bring the blessings of salvation in this life. I suppose this is true. But why should we assume that the church will be more motivated to bring *these* blessings to people than they are to bring the blessing

3. Ibid., 226.
4. Ibid.

of eternal life? The risk I am willing to take to save a person from execution is not increased by telling me, "He is no longer on death row, but surely you will want to feel all the same urgency to help him find a good life."

4. Finally, Ellenberger argues that believing some are saved apart from the preaching of the gospel "reaffirms love as the primary motivation."[5] Again this is unintelligible to me, since it seems to assume that the urgency of missions driven by the desire to rescue people from eternal torment is not love. How does saying some are saved without the gospel make a greater appeal to love?

So I affirm again that the abandonment of the universal necessity of hearing the gospel for salvation does indeed diminish the urgency of world evangelization. And I say again that this is *not* the main reason for affirming the necessity of hearing and believing the gospel for salvation. The main reason is that the Bible teaches it, and therefore the good of man and the glory of God are most honored by it.

"Let Us Go with Him Outside the Camp"

Therefore, the church is bound to engage with the Lord of glory in his cause. Charles Hodge is right that "the solemn question, implied in the language of the apostle, HOW CAN THEY BELIEVE WITHOUT A

5. Ibid.

PREACHER? should sound day and night in the ears of the churches."[6] It is our unspeakable privilege to be caught up with him in the greatest movement in history—the ingathering of the elect "from every tribe and language and people and nation" until the full number of the Gentiles come in, and all Israel is saved, and the Son of Man descends with power and great glory as King of kings and Lord of lords, and the earth is full of the knowledge of his glory as the waters cover the sea forever and ever (Hab. 2:14). Then the supremacy of Christ will be manifest to all, and he will deliver the kingdom to God the Father, and God will be all in all.

This is our final destiny. Missions is our temporary, lifelong task. Persecution may be our appointed lot (1 Thess. 3:3). Only God's approval matters in the end. "Therefore let us go to him outside the camp and bear the reproach he endured. For here we have no lasting city, but we seek the city that is to come" (Heb. 13:13–14).

6. Charles Hodge, *Commentary on the Epistle to the Romans*, 553.

John Piper (DrTheol, University of Munich) is the pastor for preaching and vision at Bethlehem Baptist Church in Minneapolis, Minnesota, where he has served since 1980. He is the author of more than forty books (including *Desiring God*, *The Pleasures of God*, and *Let the Nations Be Glad!*), and thirty years of his preaching and teaching is available at www .DesiringGod.org. John and his wife, Noel, have four sons, one daughter, and an increasing number of grandchildren.

A Note on Resources

❊ desiringGod

If you would like to explore further the vision of God and life presented in this book, we at Desiring God would love to serve you. We have hundreds of resources to help you grow in your passion for Jesus Christ and help you spread that passion to others. At our website, www.DesiringGod.org, you will find almost everything John Piper has written and preached, including more than thirty books. We have made over twenty-five years of sermons available free online for you to read, listen to, download, and in some cases watch. In addition, you can access hundreds of articles, listen to our daily internet radio program, find out where John Piper is speaking, learn about our conferences, discover our God-centered children's curricula, and browse our online store. John Piper receives no royalties from the books he writes and no compensation from Desiring God. The funds are all reinvested into our efforts to spread the gospel. Desiring God also has a whatever-you-can-afford policy, designed for individuals with limited discretionary funds. If you would like more information about this policy, please contact us at the address or phone number below. We exist to help you treasure Jesus Christ and his gospel above all things because he is most glorified in you when you are most satisfied in him. Let us know how we can serve you!

Desiring God
P.O. Box 2901
Minneapolis, Minnesota 55402
888-346-4700
mail@DesiringGod.org
www.DesiringGod.org